THE VIEW FROM THE FOLDING CHAIRS

BY MICHALA MILLER

WESTERN REFLECTIONS PUBLISHING COMPANY

Montrose, Colorado

First Edition
Printed in the United States of America

ISBN 1-890437-57-3
Library of Congress Catalog Number 2001116790

All illustrations by Jean Kashner © 2001
Cover and text design by Laurie Goralka Design

Western Reflections Publishing Company
P.O. Box 1647
Montrose, CO 81402-1647
www.westernreflectionspub.com

❯ Dedicated to all my family ❮

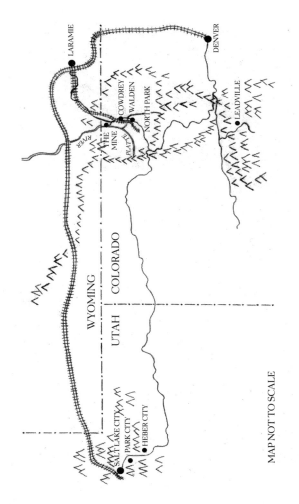

MAP AREA AS IT WAS IN THE 1940s

LARAMIE

DENVER

COWDREY
WALDEN
NORTH PARK
THE
MINE
PLATTE
RIVER

LEADVILLE

WYOMING

COLORADO

UTAH

SALT LAKE CITY
PARK CITY
HEBER CITY

MAP NOT TO SCALE

❧ Contents ❧

❧ PREFACE ❧

I squeezed on the wad of tinfoil in my pocket. It represented weeks of reclaiming bits and pieces of shiny foil from gum wrappers, lids and trash piles. Into the grocery store I went, and there, on the counter next to the cash register, was a gallon-sized, glass pickle jar half full of tin-foil. I proudly opened the lid and added my silvery contribution.

Though far from the shooting, far from the military bases, and far from the war factories, I wasn't far from the war. In 1938, when I was five years old, a dark shroud cloaked the world. It was not cast aside until August of 1945.

World War II must remain a time in history never to be forgotten or glossed over. Historians have recorded the battles, the heroes, the destruction. My reflections are of my wartime life in a high mountain plateau in northern Colorado, where my father operated a flourspar mine. This essential war time mineral was used in hydrofluoric acid and as a flux in steel to take out the impurities.

My summers were spent on the mine ranch, owned for its water rights and leased to a ranching family. There in a former roadhouse for wagon and buggy travelers of another time, I lived out the summers of the war.

The winters were spent in a warmer, more modern, rented house in the town of Walden, population six hundred, some sixteen miles from the mine. Walden was the center of the county and of my world.

In the years from 1941 to 1945, we were a country united a people committed, a spirit determined. All did small things for a larger purpose, and I was one of them. My contributions, for the most part, were a series of missteps such as a knitted afghan, full of holes, for a cold and suffering serviceman. The war stamps I bought weren't from self-sacrifice but because the store candy cases were empty.

World War II ended over half a century ago, but the impressions those years made have lingered throughout my life.

⋇ Hard Times ⋇

I leaned out of the open car window to get a glimpse of the army crossing our neighbor's land. They trudged slowly across the field, leaning forward with heads bent, their hats pulled down to protect them from the sun and the wind that blew more often than not.

I was disappointed. From the way my parents had spoken I expected the Civilian Conservation Corps (CCC), started by the government in 1937 to provide jobs, to be hundreds of soldiers with flags and guns invading our ranch land. Instead there were fewer than fifty men pouring poison down prairie dog holes. There was nothing snappy or military as they moved, a few yards apart, across the mound-filled pasture. They started, stopped, opened their bags, bent over, poured, straightened and moved on.

I felt no pain for the prairie dogs. They ruined good land. I knew of more than one horse that had to be shot because of a broken leg caused from stepping in a dog's hole. It wasn't that I disliked prairie dogs, in fact, their "attention and on guard" posture from atop their mounds was far more military than that of the plodding men. The CCC were just men who had a job to do. They came and left and offered very little excitement. They were part of a time when people, so to speak, "made do."

Times were hard I'd been told and, while my folks didn't dwell on it, I knew we had more than most people. My father had a job. This became apparent to me when men stopped at our house and asked for food. Although we couldn't wait to tell Dad a bum had come, we didn't think of him as any less a person. Bum was just a word for someone walking and asking for food, and besides, Mother always treated them with respect.

We had a "bum procedure" that we followed. When one walked by and turned down our road, we knew we had to go inside. With my older sister, Margaret, and I hiding behind her, Mother met him at the door and offered him a meal. She didn't let him come in but asked the man to wait on the porch, which was attached to the east side of the house where the hill dropped off. By sitting on the edge of the porch, it was a comfortable place to rest and dangle my feet; I liked to swing mine back and forth. A few feet beyond the weathered porch was the worn path over the hill to the outhouse and beyond that the pasture, the creek and Sentinel Mountain.

From the living room window we spied on the stranger, while Mother usually fried bacon or ham and two eggs. She made several pieces of toast and served the breakfast on the family dishes, complete with napkin and a large white mug of coffee.

While we watched through the lace curtains, Mother carried the meal to the porch. After setting it down, she asked about home and family, and often mentioned that she was from southern Illinois, Elizabethtown, on the Ohio River. She visited a few more minutes and then left the bum to eat. She returned several more times to fill the mug, while we checked out the bum's manners and speculated on what he might have been before hard times.

I wanted my mother to tell the wanderer that it was a long way between people, that there were no houses over the mountain pass, and not many cars went by, but Mother didn't talk about bad things.

Many folks nearby were suffering during those late Depression years. One hard-up family that I knew stayed for a time in a black, tar-papered cabin at the mine. They lived on whistle pigs—marmots. I had no desire to eat those larger, fatter members of the rodent family but neither was I appalled at someone else trying them.

The family had several children. One boy, named Rick, hiked around the mountain to play with us. He was always welcome, and while we gave him lunch and played together, we were never out of range of Mother's watchful eye. He was older but I suspect no wiser. Rick and his family lived rent-free at the mine, but by fall they found the cabin too cold and moved on, or maybe they just got tired of whistle pigs. Whatever the reason we missed our friend. Playmates were scarce.

Mother did her best to fill our days and that included teaching us how to embroider. Although I hated to sew, I looked forward to the late summer afternoons when my mother, my sister and I sat on three folding chairs on the porch and embroidered pillowcases. Mother usually did two cases a summer and my sister completed one. I never managed to finish mine, but I didn't mind sleeping on a few less French knots. The joy was in looking up the valley, seeing the road disappear into the canyon and visiting. The topics of conversation I no longer remember; but they were probably whatever girls, seven and nine, liked to talk about.

Some afternoons Mother even attempted to teach us how to play bridge, a card game she dearly loved. The lessons weren't entirely successful; but I did learn how to deal, count trump and not cry when I lost.

It was during one of those summer months that a large map appeared on the wall above our battery-operated radio. This map of Europe held something of a place of honor and much attention was paid to it. It was later joined by another map, this one of the Pacific. From the earliest rumblings of war my parents followed the exploits of a man named Hitler on the Atlas. For five or six years these two maps were covered with pins to show battles won, rivers crossed, islands lost and countries defeated. Like the radio, the two played an important part in our lives.

I felt the tension within my parents as they listened to the news and marched the pins back and forth across the maps. Something told me there were harder times ahead.

❧ Coupons ❧

War meant coupons for shoes, coupons for gasoline, and coupons for food. Rationing was a way of life and coupon books were a familiar sight, for having the money to buy a steak meant nothing without the right number of coupons. It was wartime, a time of shortages and sacrificing. It took constant vigilance, a creative mind, and hard work to juggle living with coupons and providing what my sister and I were told were well-balanced meals. Fresh fruits and vegetables were in short supply and trips to the grocery store were infrequent.

My mother discovered that canned hominy required fewer coupons than other canned vegetables, and a week never passed that didn't include at least one hominy dish. How I hated those roundish, whitish, slickish kernels that grew on my spoon from my plate to my mouth. No seasoning, home-canned tomatoes or other disguise covered that disgusting feeling as my teeth sliced into them.

To save those precious coupons, my sister and I fished the stream below our summer home for trout.

Although we liked to fish, when it meant having to catch a "mess" for supper, the sport lost some of its luster. As the summer progressed, digging fish worms presented a challenge. This elusive bait was hard to find in the dry soil, and we resorted to digging in the chicken house where it was cooler, the soil richer and somewhat moist.

If the fish were biting, we saved on worms by using a caught fish's eyes as bait. Other times, when we had lost most of our worms to snags and wily fish, we were forced to pinch the worms in half. Then we stretched the amputated remains tight as we threaded the hook, even though we knew a pleated worm was more delectable to a brook trout.

As the water dropped in late summer, we resorted to fishing the beaver dams where we sat behind the willows with our lines draped over the limbs. There we waited, hoping a fish would bite, until, after awhile, we gave up and tried another familiar hole. Finally, we trudged back up the hill and, if we were lucky, Mother cleaned our trout. If not, we spread out newspaper and using a pair of scissors cut the fish's belly from tail to gills. Then we reached in, grabbed the gills and yanked downward, pulling out all the guts in one motion. Next we washed the fish in a pan of cold water, checked to make sure we'd stripped them clean, and laid the "mess" side by side so we could argue over who had caught the biggest.

Most of the time the fish were eight to ten inches long with firm, bright pink meat. When rolled in corn meal and fried they were delicious, plus they saved on coupons.

To help out the meat situation, we also raised chickens during the summer. Our coop wasn't much, and frequently the skunks ate more chicken than we did, but those fryers that made it to the table were much appreciated.

One moment in our chicken raising history made me very proud of my mother. It was towards the end of a summer, and we had two chickens left to eat. They were wild, flying in and out of the limp wire-and-slab chicken pen at will. They were slated for dinner along with corn bread, mashed potatoes and gravy, sliced tomatoes, and pie. That day, with Mother waving her apron, we were able to corner one chicken between the outhouse and what had once been a sawed-log garage.

The second chicken had a mind of its own, and while Mother hauled the caught chicken to the chopping block by the woodshed, my sister and I chased the other squawking bird around the coop, behind the outhouse, and past the garage. Mother put the first chicken's head between two nails driven into the end of the block, gave one swing of the ax, and the chicken was flapping headless on the ground. She snatched it up, retrieved a teakettle of boiling water from the kitchen, poured boiling water on the luckless bird, plucked it, and finally lit a cone-shaped roll of newspaper to singe off any remaining feathers.

By now we were tiring out and the remaining chicken was headed for the pasture between our house and Pinkham Creek. The hay crew for the ranch had come in for lunch and joined in the chase. Maybe number two chicken had seen what had happened to number one, for it raced wildly along the fence, through the grass, and around the willows.

About that time, Mother called out one of her "Yoo-hoos," and we looked up to see her standing at the brow of the hill holding Dad's 22 rifle. As she stood there in her cotton house dress and white apron, her feet were planted far apart, and that meant only one thing. She'd had enough of that loose chicken. She waved us aside, took aim at the racing chicken and fired.

To the amazement of the teenage hay hands, the chicken suddenly stopped running and flopped over in its tracks. When we examined it, that hen was missing most of her head. House dress, apron or not, that was some shot, and those hay hands were impressed. I insisted on carrying the chicken up the hill and handed it to my mother with a flourish, but she was in no humor for theatrics, and set off to treat this chicken to the same fate as the first. It wouldn't be long before we ate those renegades.

In the meantime, we sat on the folding chairs on the porch, caught our breath, and relived what was an exciting event in our quiet lives.

❧ Paper Day ❧

Thursday was paper day, the day the local, weekly newspaper came out. The Jackson County Star and Thursday were synonymous. It contained vital news for kids like a review of up-coming movies, or maybe we'd see our name in the school news. The weeks when they reported perfect spelling grades for the report card period my name was missing, and I didn't find it under the most book reports either, but it was on the list of cast members for the musical production, *Jack and the Bean Stalk*. I was the rear end of Jack's cow and performed a little soft shoe.

After the war began the first and second columns on the left-hand side of the front page were the most read. They contained information about and letters from our servicemen and women. For such a sparsely populated area perhaps more than our share joined the armed services, including some young cowboys or hay hands that had come to work on the ranches. It didn't matter to us that they were "outsiders," a term we used for anyone who came from somewhere else. Following the letter from one of them, the editor would add a sentence saying which ranch he had worked on.

All the letters were eagerly read and almost always they were cheerful and had a humorous line or two. The writer frequently thanked the editor for his or her free weekly copy, which cost the rest of us a nickel. A sailor wrote that when he got back to port he had a big surprise-there were five newspapers waiting for him. Another mentioned seeing a friend from North Park in a canteen in Scotland. In such a big world I found that hard to imagine.

One of our airmen scolded us in his letter from England, "Talk about rationing, you don't know anything about rationing, everything is rationed here and they don't complain." I wondered if that meant the movies-surely not!

A family that worked for the railroad dropped their son's letter by for the editor to print. He published a few lines that brought tears to my mother's eyes. He had written, "Don't worry. I got hit by a sniper bullet. It went in under my jaw and came out the back of my neck but missed any bones. Got the Purple Heart."

I said at the supper table that evening that I thought he should have mentioned the good news first—he got a medal. My father explained you got the Purple Heart for being wounded in the service of our country. I guess the wound had to come first. Later the same soldier was awarded the Oak Leaf Cluster, which sounded like he had a second big wound.

I objected most to the censorship. The servicemen and women couldn't tell us exactly where they were, what they were doing, or who they had shot at. We never read about the good stuff. Instead as one soldier wrote, "I'm somewhere in the East Indies, traveling a lot and seeing the same scenery—snakes and bugs." I decided he was lost in a jungle.

The newspaper was more important to Mother than anyone else in the family. It was true that the editor's wife called Mother every Monday to see if she had any news, knew of anyone who was sick, or had gone "outside" to Laramie. Those general items were found in the middle of the paper. What Mother needed was information on the front page about current rationing, what stamps were useable, and for how long. She sat on a folding chair in front of the card table with the newspaper, the coupons, and her grocery list. To one side were the red coupons, which were used for red meat and fat.

Four red stamps represented forty points and had to last for five weeks. I often wandered by, looked over her shoulder, and suggested we have steak for one meal; her reply was always a deep sigh.

On the other side of the table were the blue coupons, which were spent for processed foods, such as canned spinach and that awful, low point hominy. To add to the confusion were the few separate sugar coupons. They were numbered, and one of those allowed Mother to buy five pounds of sugar. And probably somewhere in her purse were the stamps with airplanes printed on them for purchasing shoes. During the entire war my grandmother never had a new pair of shoes; she sent her coupons for my sister and me.

My father was lucky; all he had to worry about were the gasoline coupons. If the supply was shorter than usual, one coupon allowed him to buy three gallons of gas, but most of the time it was four.

About half way through the war, red and blue tokens were issued for meat and processed food. To me it was like getting change back from a coupon. To mother it was one more thing to keep track of. I soon learned not to bump the table when she was counting the tokens and coupons.

Other important information in the paper included weddings, births, meetings, and programs—even birthday parties. The day I found a brief article about an emergency landing at our airport, I was crushed. Something that important and I missed it. A "P-38" fighter plane had landed on our dirt runway because the pilot was short on fuel. Our airstrip, a mile north of town, was flat, the sagebrush had been cleared, and it had a windsock. That was about it, but then under the circumstances, the pilot couldn't be picky. He had left San Francisco heading for the East coast when he was forced to circle south because of a storm, and having used too much fuel landed in North Park. Our airport didn't have airplane gasoline, so the plane sat on the runway until a gas truck arrived from the Cheyenne, Wyoming air base.

I did get to see an army transport from Nebraska with a crew of three. They had been practicing reconnaissance flying and landed to check over their plane. My father drove us to the airport to see what was going on, but there wasn't much happening, so we didn't even get out of the car.

I was most interested in a short paragraph from the sheriff's office. They had been notified that the president of our country ordered all aliens to turn in their radios and cameras. I wasn't exactly sure what an alien was, but I kept a careful lookout for anyone suspicious. I even looked closely at the paper for several weeks hoping to read about at least one confiscated radio or camera.

The Jackson County Star informed and connected our community. When the center of the front page had a box with a small American flag in it and the name of one of our servicemen killed in action, we all hurt.

✦ SADIE ✦

What ever happened to Sadie, our commode? During the war years she held a dominant place in our family. I think my father came up with that name because it sounds to me like an Irishman's sense of humor.

We spent our summers on a ranch, in a two-story, sawed-log house, a mile from the fluorspar mine where my father worked. The mining company owned the ranch for the right to take water out of Pinkham Creek which wandered through the pasture and hay meadows. That water right provided the water to mill the ore and was as necessary as the mineral itself. This part-time home was stuck into a rather steep, treeless hillside. The thick rock foundation, holding up the large, square fortress, housed a couple of big rooms in what would now be called a walkout basement.

The main floor had four rooms separated by a long hall with two rooms of equal size on each side. The top floor had five rooms, also divided by a hall. The layout resembled a hotel, which it had been in the early 1900s. It was originally built as a stage stop where passengers spent the night on their arduous trip over the mountains from southern Wyoming into North Park, Colorado.

On the second floor was the bathroom, a twenty-five by twenty-foot room where we roller-skated. The tub with its big claw-shaped feet and high sides was so immense that two of us could disappear in it during a game of hide-and-seek. Having the room and all the plumbing fixtures didn't necessarily mean we had a working bath-room. Two floors below and beneath the staircase, in what was considered the basement, lay the remains of our rural electrical system. It had provided us with lights and pumped the water from the well until it died shortly after the war began. Repair parts and batteries weren't available. We spent the war years with an outhouse down over the hill—and Sadie.

Sadie was the utility kind of portable commode made of white enamel with matching lid and wooden handle. No matter how hard I tried, I never was able to put the lid on Sadie without making a loud clanging noise. In the middle of the night the sound of Sadie's lid clattering on the rim told the entire household someone was "up." Sadie was cold and a shock to the bottom, but that was better than the long trek, flashlight in hand, down the hill to the outhouse.

Mother was in charge of Sadie, a task I doubt that she enjoyed, for Sadie was emptied and scalded with boiling water every morning, then hidden under the porch to air until dark. Sadie was as much a part of those years as the lantern placed strategically near the center of the table, where in the evening we all sat to read: my father studying the *Wall Street Journal,* Mother with her *Denver Post,* my sister reading a library book, and a comic book for me.

Circling the light was a host of flying bugs, whatever variety that had penetrated the worn screen door, while we sat on two kitchen and two folding chairs with faces to the light and backs to the black shadows. I feared those dark silhouettes and never left the other readers until I had company. Then I took a lighted candle to the kitchen sink where I filled a cup with water from the galvanized bucket to aid in brushing my teeth. Brush, spit, sip, rinse, and repeat. Afterwards, with the flickering flame, I headed for Sadie and bed.

The rooms with their high ceilings were, even in summer, often cold, so Mother warmed irons on the stove, wrapped them in towels, and shoved one in the bottom of each bed. What a welcome sensation to extend my toes until they found the warm lump and then cup my feet around it. With blankets high and head tucked low, the cold and blackness disappeared.

After the war ended and within a few years, rural electrification brought a new way of life to our home. We had lights, a refrigerator, a new pump in the well, and we had a working bathroom.

The last I remember of Sadie she was tucked away under the porch step. The mining company eventually sold the ranch, and we gave up our summer home. Some years later the old landmark was torn down. I wonder what ever happened to Sadie?

❧ WASH DAY ❧

Doing the laundry was a family affair during the summer. In a dark corner of the basement next to a thick rock foundation was an ice cold shallow well. We never drank the water but rather walked to the outdoor well some distance from our house. The basement well provided water for the washing machine and two rinse tubs. Chiseled into the wall next to the well was a ledge with a niche that held our bottles of milk and a package or two of meat. It was the only refrigerator we had.

Early Monday morning my father built a fire in the small basement stove. It was close to the floor but had a wide flat stovetop and two lids to feed the fire. When it got hot he filled from the well an oval shaped boiler that just covered the stove. As the water heated he filled one rinse tub half full with cold water and the other tub almost to the top. These tubs were positioned so the ringer swung over them and reached the wicker clothes basket. Then he started the gas motor that ran the machine and headed off to the mine for work.

Now it was my mother's turn as she carried all the dirty laundry down the stairs and divided it into piles of white, colored, and work clothes. She dipped the hot water with a bucket and dumped it into the machine and finished filling the first rinse tub.

I liked to watch as she shaved a bar of P&G soap into the washer. If I was lucky she let me pull the black knob back that started the agitator. I pretended it was the gearshift on our car.

As the soap dissolved and the bubbles rose Mother pushed the sheets into the water. We weren't allowed to operate the ringer, a piece of equipment that fascinated me. Mother had heard too many stories about fingers, hands and arms crushed between the two rollers.

While the loads made their way from tub to basket more piles disappeared into the machine. Mother hung out the sheets, but after that my sister and I did the rest. Our two clotheslines were long, but they also went down a rather steep hill. It took care and agility to keep the basket upright on the ground and maintain our balance as we stretched to pin what I thought was an endless amount of wash.

When all the tubs were finally empty of laundry and the full lines sagged with their load, we were free to play till it was time "to gather." Mother swept the basement and then drained the tubs, using some of the water to swab the rough floor.

While the bright sun and stiff breeze did their job, Mother had a few minutes to take tablet and pencil to the front porch where she sat on a folding chair writing her weekly letter to my grandmother. Every Monday Mother wrote, every Tuesday the letter was mailed and every Friday we got a letter back. My Grandmother's letters always started with the salutation, "Dearest little family." If a letter was late getting posted, which was rare, or we didn't have one on the appointed day, it was cause for alarm.

It was next to impossible to make a phone call to my grandmother, so all of our lives and love were conveyed on those lined pages. I knew little about the Illinois relatives and since my mother was an only child, these great aunts and uncles with names like Evie, Daisy, and Dewey brought no memories to my mind. But I understood that they were important to Mother.

Long before I was ready, we were called to gather the clothes off the line and help with the folding. The next day the important pieces would be sprinkled, wrapped in a towel, and ironed. I never got to sprinkle since I didn't sprinkle but rather drowned the cotton. I did iron my own jeans and shirts. The irons were heated on the back of the stove and retrieved with a detachable wooden handle. It seemed to me that it was very easy to scorch my part.

As the day wore down we expected leftovers for supper, a Monday ritual, and knew that we'd all go to bed before long.

❧ MY WAR EFFORT ❧

I collected bits of tinfoil, which I wadded into a ball and dropped in the gallon jar on the counter at the grocery store. Everyone saved foil. I went in search of old rubber tires, long ago forgotten along irrigation ditches, on old trash piles, or in the gullies. Everyone searched for rubber. Since the Japanese had captured the rubber plantations of Sumatra, our country was desperate for rubber. I even gave up a rubber doll, which was of no great loss to me. I had poured milk into it, and ever after a sour odor remained.

I bought war stamps, licked them, and stuck them on the pages in the paper booklet. When it was filled with the $18.50 worth of stamps, I turned it in for a $25 war bond. It took a long, long time for me to fill one book. Everyone bought and licked stamps.

We even had bond raffles where we gathered at the community hall to raffle off such things as an oil change, five gallons of gas, or even a couple dozen fresh eggs. My mother bought a round, frosted glass cake plate at the drug store gift counter to be raffled off at such an occasion.

"Mike," she said to my father, "you buy that cake platter." He wanted the oil change but instead bought a fifty-dollar bond, which included the plate, and from then on it was in the center of the table whenever we had an important birthday celebration. Everyone bought bonds.

But not everyone made an afghan for the war effort. I "sort of" did. It was a painful experience and not one I'm proud to talk about. A local sweater knitter, I don't remember who, got together a group of girls to create an afghan for a cold, suffering serviceman. Five or six of us sat on folding chairs around a card table loaded with rulers, balls of drab brown yarn, and pairs of knitting needles. From the table we were given one of each of the aforementioned items.

The knitting lady had cast on each pair of needles about twenty-five stitches. The goal was a six-inch knitted square with a further goal of each of us making at least six squares. When the blocks were completed, we would sew them together and send off to the Red Cross a warm, wonderful cover.

I knew from the very beginning I was in trouble as the teacher explained and demonstrated each knitting step. I held the needles awkwardly in my hands, and pressed the ball of yarn between my legs so it couldn't fall to the floor. I jammed the needle under the first stitch, wrapped the yarn around it, pulled it through, and transferred the new stitch to the other needle. I struggled with each stitch until the yarn became limp, damp and twisted. At the end of the row, I was missing stitches and holes appeared in their places.

Slow and tortured was my progress. I learned, however, after every few rows, to hold the loaded needle between my teeth and pull with both hands on the knitting. That way it stretched to the six-inch requirement without my having to knit as many rows. Never mind that between the dropped stitches and the tugging, the square looked like a crocheted doily.

After a few sessions, the knitting coach ignored me. I never completed my required six squares, and when it was time to sew it together, I was thankfully overlooked. I didn't mind since I had a feeling no soldier would crawl under the ugly thing no matter how cold it got. I quickly forgot the knitting fiasco and hoped the "afghan lady" would forget me if she found more yarn.

What I considered my greatest war effort was not the foil balls nor an afghan, but when I gave up my father for many months. Our government needed him elsewhere. He was too old for the draft but, like many civilians, he went wherever he was called. Through a long winter I waited while he put into operation a fluorspar mill in northern New Mexico. Fluorspar, a variegated green, purple, and white mineral, was used as a flux in making steel and in hydrofluoric acid.

I missed him. When I complained about his being gone so long from home, my mother said, "Think of all the children whose fathers are fighting for us overseas."

What more could I say?

❖ More Things Patriotic ❖

Less than two months into the war, a sign appeared on Main Street. It wasn't the result of debate and consent by the town fathers or the civic program of a service organization but rather the initiative of a local businessman. He cut a large "V" from a piece of thick plywood. Two men that worked for the city picked up the "V" and took it to the town power plant where they painted it with aluminum paint and attached colored light bulbs around the edges. When completed it was hoisted up and hooked to an electric pole in a prominent place in front of a liquor store-about in the center of town.

As I was taking a short cut through the alley I spied the red, white, and blue lights surrounding the silvery "V." I ran to the pole and stood beneath it, gazing upward in awe at the symbol of victory. Little did I know how long the "V" would remain a beacon in our little town.

While the "V" stirred our patriotism, one of the more concrete efforts was the scrap metal drive.

These drives were announced in the paper several weeks ahead of time. The designated place was a vacant lot behind the corner general store. Just before the scrap was to be shipped out, I'd wander by to see how much metal had been dropped off. The lot was usually full of twisted piles, and I knew that as many as three railroad cars were needed to haul it all away. The mine sent in at least a dump truck full. If the drive was in the spring, the truck, after dumping the load, swung by our home to move our hefty, upright piano to the ranch house for the summer where I was expected to keep practicing. More than once the piano banged against the side of the truck or was dropped when loading and unloading. Through the years chunks were knocked from its sides. It had to be tuned whenever a tuner could be found. The rest of the time, I played on it, hardly noticing that it was out of key.

I didn't take part in the scrap drives but was involved in all the tin collections. After we hammered the last ooze from the toothpaste tube, I returned it to the drug store where the pharmacist had a collection bucket. Sometimes I added a zinc oxide tube or one from another type of ointment, but mostly it was toothpaste. It was a small contribution; however, with everyone doing it the country a noticeable amount of tin was saved.

On a much grander scale were the War Chest Loans where the citizens of our country bought government war bonds to help pay for the war. Throughout the four war years I remember seven such drives, but there may have been more. The counties were assigned quotas for the bond sales, and we were always over the top, once by three hundred percent-a figure I couldn't comprehend. After each successful campaign a Victory Dance was held with the music donated by our local musicians. They usually charged men and couples ninety-nine cents to get in, but single ladies were free.

Although they were called public dances they were more like a community party. As the evening progressed small children fell asleep on piles of coats or under folding chairs in the corners. My father dutifully pushed me around the floor a few times pumping my arm up and down and doing what was called the two-step. I frequently danced with a classmate, and often I danced with another girl on a section of the dance floor not frequented by the adults. We tried to jitterbug, step, step, and a "quick, quick," as we did our best to mimic this lively dance of the times.

If it was my lucky night I was on the floor with a male partner when someone took over the "mike" at the bandstand to call a round dance. Then we all joined hands, man on the left, woman on the right, and formed a big circle. The circle shuffled left a dozen feet and then circled right. We chained hand over hand, "Ladies south and gents north," until the caller ordered, "Dance with your new partner." We danced, promenaded, circled, and changed partners again, until the caller thought it was time for some noise. Next came the best part of the round dance as we ran, hands held high toward the center with everyone yelling. We backed out, and if our hollering wasn't loud enough we were instructed to do it again. The end of the round dance produced much confusion when the caller shouted, "Find your original partner." To me it was a good round dance if it lasted a long time and I danced with a number of partners without stepping on anyone's feet.

The Victory Dance, like all dances, ended with the playing of "Goodnight, Sweetheart." Most of the time I was at home in bed long before that familiar piece.

❧ THE PARADE ❧

While all community functions took a back seat to the war effort, there were traditions that continued, such as the summer parade and rodeo. To say they were even smaller than usual is an understatement, but they happened.

The year I was in Camp Fire Girls I was in the parade. We made elaborate preparations which included driving into the forest to collect pine boughs and a few small trees. We each brought along a brown sack lunch, and I got to take my father's hatchet. I was very proud of the red handled, leather cased hatchet-until I attempted to use it. When my father chopped kindling, it looked so easy. It took only a shaky "whack" or two before a mother took over and I became, to my relief, a bough collector.

On the morning of the parade, we met at our leader's house dressed in blue jeans and white blouses. It might have been disloyal but I was wearing my brown Girl Scout shoes—the only shoes I owned.

We used baling wire to attach the boughs along the sides of a flatbed truck and wired the trees to the back of the cab. In this woodland scene we all sat cross-legged around a pretend fire in the center of the bed. The rear of our float was adorned with a homemade banner made of butcher paper. Tacked between the brake lights it stated our name, which was something like Chicaboo, plus in smaller letters, "Camp Fire Girls."

The business part of town was about two blocks long, but the parade route started at the community church, and by the time we had gone down the main street and doubled back we'd covered at least eight blocks.

First marched the flag bearers, followed by the rodeo queen and her lady-in-waiting riding palomino horses. Next came the band, which consisted of a handful of high school musicians riding in the back of a pickup, and behind them the floats. The parade was composed of three so-called floats: a woman's organization, a load of logs headed for the sawmill, and we "Camp Firers." The remainder of the parade was made up of horses and riders. Even some very small children rode with a parent holding a lead rope. Lots of horses, usually four or six abreast, passed in review, many of which would make a second appearance that afternoon at the rodeo. Without the four-legged animals, it wouldn't have been much of a parade.

Three men were picked at random to be the float judges, and that year my father was picked. He used the term "railroaded into it," but since no one objected to his obvious conflict of interest, he had the job. The judges stood in front of the bar about half way down the block and across from the drug store. They faced west so that the morning sun was not in their eyes while they judged, or maybe that was just where the three of them met.

Mine was the first float, right behind the musical pickup, and we got lots of applause. Next was the load of logs with the driver waving and honking his horn and, finally the third bunch, the "women's group," who tried to sing as they passed in review. They were also on a flatbed truck sitting on folding chairs and wearing old-fashioned dresses. One woman worked a butter churn, shoving the plunger up and down, while another sat at an old treadle sewing machine. Their theme must have been pioneer women, but the judges weren't too impressed for we got first prize and five dollars for our coffer. Second prize caused a problem when one of the judges voted for the load of logs.

"The women will be mad as hell if we put the load of logs ahead of them," argued the other two.

Wisdom prevailed with three dollars and second prize going to the pioneer float, and a buck for third prize landed in the pocket of the driver of the load of logs. Several ranchers along the sidewalk commented on the good looking horseflesh parading by, but horses didn't compete for the money.

All too soon the parade was over. Everyone stood around for at least an hour to visit. Visiting time was almost as scarce as gasoline and parades. I may have helped remove the boughs from the flatbed but, more likely, I was doing my share of the talking. A free day in town with lots of folks to share it was rare.

❧ Pets ❧

There were rumbles and grumbles, which my father ignored, but when they continued he said to my mother, "The miners are losing things from the change room." She asked if they were suspicious of anyone.

"Well there's one miner who's fairly new and they've mentioned him. But then he isn't well liked to start out with." He paused, "Now that I think about it, the stealing began after he came to work here."

"What has he taken?"

"It hasn't amounted to much until yesterday," said my father. "It was change, quarters and dimes, a pocket knife, but now a watch is missing."

One of the oldest buildings at the mine was the blacksmith shop. It was just east of the tunnel portal and constructed of the usual rough boards and tarpaper. It was also the change room for the miners where they left their lunch pails, good clothes, and valuables. I was only allowed in there with my father when all the men where underground. It wasn't much of a place, just a couple of "barny" rooms, and I'd rather walk the mine rails or stand in the cool entrance to the tunnel. That is until it was obvious that there was a thief among us, and then I followed closely all the news from the mine. Each week something was missing, and finally the "suspicious one" was confronted. He denied that he was stealing and pushed away his accuser. A fight was in progress when the underground foreman stepped between them. A day or two later, when the foreman heard that a silver spoon from a leftover lunch had disappeared, he thought he could solve the crime. He brought a ladder from the warehouse and climbed up to check the rafters. It wasn't long before he found all the stolen items. In a dark corner tucked beneath the roof was a pack rat's nest filled with shiny items.

After every one got their missing things back there was talk of shooting or trapping the pack rat. Instead they gave him a name, Johnny; and he became something of a pet. From then on the miners kept any thing that glistened undercover and left bits of food on the bench for Johnny. Soon the rat got braver, and I spent time in the change room looking for him. Usually I only saw his long tail wrapped over a rafter and hanging down. But at other times he ran along the boards beneath the roof peering down with tiny eyes as shiny as all the things he had stolen.

While Johnny was an elusive pet, Cheekee was ever present. She arrived at the mine by way of a couple that worked on the railroad. They looked out their window one late spring morning and, to their amazement, saw a fawn nursing from one of their goats. No one knew where the baby deer had come from, but all assumed that the mother deer had been killed during hunting season. The fawn was eventually dropped off at the mine where Cheekee, named by the railroaders, became a member of the camp. She liked her having ears scratched, cigarettes to eat, and to be in the middle of a crowd.

The powerhouse, the bunkhouse, and the cookhouse all resounded with the same order, "Close the door, here comes Cheekee!" She was known to follow the men into the office knocking over folding chairs and shelves made from stacked dynamite boxes. When they were signing their time cards she pushed her way up to the counter; and if Cheekee felt left out, she put a hoof on the shoulder of one of the men and peered over his head.

The following hunting season there was much concern for the deer's safety. Because penning a deer was illegal, Cheekee was decked out in yards and yards of red cheesecloth. It hung around her neck like a flaming garland and waved almost to the ground between her front legs. While most of the workers went hunting-many not far from the mine buildings-the thought of anyone taking a shot at Cheekee was appalling. She escaped the season unscathed and hung around the mine for another six months. Then one day she was missing. We were convinced she had gone back into the woods and assured ourselves it was "as nature intended." But we missed her, and I never saw her again. However some mill workers were outside one day when they spotted a deer and her fawn on the skyline. They yelled, "Come Cheekee, Come!"

She came. She left her fawn under some brush and taking her usual dainty steps came down the haul road to the men. She was greeted enthusiastically, given cigarettes, pats, and scratches. Cheekee remained for half an hour or so then left as if called. She jumped over the sagebrush and made her way to the brow of the hill. She never came back.

COATS AND
❧ COLORING BOOKS ❧

The remoteness of our area and its sparse population brought with it the added responsibility of taking care of each other, and this responsibility was made clear to me at an early age.

My sister and I got new winter coats every two years. The first winter the coats were near ankle length and only the tips of our fingers peeked out of the sleeves. They were made of thick wool to handle our long, cold and windy winters, and we bore their weight, whether it was to school, to play, or for dress. By the end of the second year the sleeves were too short, the collars a little worn and the cold wrapped around our exposed knees.

One fall, after the first big snow, we were walking to our piano lessons when I spotted my last year's coat on a child, and my sister's coat on her sister.

"Hey look," I said, "there's my old coat."

A vise-like grip numbed my arm, and I knew my mother wanted my attention right then and there. She bent over and, in a low voice that commanded my greatest respect, she informed me that I was never to say anything about that coat to anyone. I never did. As time passed, I often noticed my old clothes and my friend's clothes in someone else's wardrobe. It didn't mean we were giving to the poor or for that matter even helping out. It was just what everyone did.

Then there was the time my mother gave away one of the few jackets I'd ever owned, and I rather resented that act of kindness. My grandmother had sent me a leather jacket, a leftover from her general store in Illinois. It was too big, stiff, and lined with a slick fabric that "zapped" me with an electrical shock when I stuck my arms through the sleeves. I didn't even care for its dark brown color and rarely put it on.

One night the sheriff stopped to say there was a woman walking through our county, headed for Wyoming. "She's crazy," he said. "Won't ride with anyone."

It was early summer, the breeze bore a chill, and Wyoming didn't even begin for another ten miles, so out the door went my leather jacket. We heard later that the sheriff followed the crazy woman, his headlights showing her the way, clear to the Wyoming line where someone else took over.

I went to bed with a sour look on my face, but as I lay in the dark between the flannel sheets with a warmed iron wrapped at my feet, I thought about the woman. She was all alone, going somewhere, trudging mile after mile in my leather jacket. I hoped she stuck her hands in the pockets and kept warm. I hoped she got where she wanted to go, and the jacket made her life a little better. I even hoped it wouldn't "zap" her.

That jacket was soon forgotten, and now I can remember only one time when my mother's generosity was almost more than I could bear. We were at the community church's Christmas party, put on by the Ladies Aid Society of which my mother was a member. We sat in rows of folding chairs at one end of the high-ceilinged church hall, while at the opposite end was the decorated tree, and in the middle was the heating stove. Following the games and refreshments, we each received a gift that was bought, wrapped, and hidden by our mothers until it was secretly dropped beneath the tree.

I was very fortunate for I unwrapped two coloring books, one a nondescript collection of wheelbarrows, wagons and farm animals, while the other was a work of art. It had chipmunks living in tree houses, running chipmunk stores, and attending school among the branches. Each page was wonderful. As I was admiring my gifts, the child behind me began to cry. I guess her mother hadn't come or her gift was lost. Anyway, before I could protest, my beloved chipmunk coloring book was given away. It hurt for a little while, but that was how it was. We took care of each other.

It seemed like I did all the giving, but then I remember all the times I was on the receiving end. The patriotic school program was a good example. I was chosen to be Betsy Ross, a non-speaking, non-moving part. Even if my part was small, my mother's task was formidable since she had to produce the costume. How she must have dreaded the school programs! Of all her talents sewing wasn't one of them, so Mother resorted to borrowing, which meant calling and calling until she found something that "might work."

For Betsy Ross, she located a heavy black taffeta skirt further weighted down with a large rolled hem that dragged the ground. After a few airings on the clothesline and a touch-up with the iron, the skirt took on a majestic look. The loaned blouse had rows of narrow lace that covered it from its high collar to the end of its tapered bodice. This blouse had spent many years in a trunk, and belonged to a ranching friend whom we called Auntie Bess. I knew this was a special blouse just by the way I had to put it on, arms up and hands carefully worked into the sleeves. Finally a slow slide over my head and the blouse inched downward to my waist. With my hair pulled up into a bun and my borrowed clothes, I was confident that I was an elegant Betsy Ross.

On stage, the black skirt swirled around the legs of the folding chair and hid my brown Girl Scout shoes. The flag of our country rested on my lap as I pretended to stitch.

If borrowing the clothes wasn't enough, I also sold their owners tickets to the production, and they endured an evening of the red, white and blue.

❧ HALLOWEEN PARTY ❧

The Parent-Teacher Association (PTA) was alive but not very well during the war years. It didn't seem to meet very often, but instead their efforts were planned over the telephone. I know that is how my mother was put in charge of the school's Halloween party. I doubt that she volunteered; but when selected she organized, called, and with the aid of a few other mothers, produced their spookiest best.

Held in the grade school gym at a fairly early hour, so there was time afterwards for trick or treating, the party began with the overhead lights extinguished. The only light came from Jack-o'-lanterns sitting on folding chairs and floor lamps with sheets covering them. Many homes were missing their tall living room reading lamps so the gymnasium could resemble a ghost convention. I helped Mother toss the sheets over the shades making sure they reached the floor. Then we pinned on black construction paper eyes where we thought the face might be.

Streamers of black and orange crepe paper dangled over the windows, draped the walls, and drooped from stretched wire. In one corner, on a braided rug to absorb the spills, sat the traditional, galvanized tub. Filled with water and small, red apples, it was a must for any fall party.

Hidden behind a trio of lampshades, a young violin student, complete with violin and music, performed. Mother had been on one of her long walks, and when passing the violinist's house, heard her practicing. Mother walked up to the door, and right on the spot she was invited to practice during the party. The frequent softball player and sometime musician practiced her music, staring intently through the gloom at her sheet music. The bow jerked back and forth. Wails, squawks, screeches, and shrieks resounded off the cement walls and filled the party guests with giggles. I even thought I saw some trepidation. It was my mother's finest creative touch to what was a successfully, scary evening.

We dunked, ate doughnuts off a string, and paraded in our homemade costumes. There was an abundance of bums, cowboys, and ghosts with a smattering of witches and princesses. I wore my usual miner's outfit composed of a hard hat, carbide lamp, and pick. Then dessert was served and the party was over. To me, the only drawback to the evening was the dessert. I wasn't fond of orange Jello and the dollop of whipped cream on top was more than I could handle. Jello was standard because it didn't need sugar and many of our homes had no refrigerators. We even had Jello for birthdays. I was saved by the square of cake, also donated by the "committee." There were white cakes, pink cakes, and even a devil's food cake as well as ours.

My mother's cake was legendary—a delicate chocolate with a velvet grain and topped with a creamy, fudge frosting. Whether it was a birth, death, or somewhere in between, she showed up with that brown cake. I don't know how many times I offered to bring the Kool-Aid or chips to a "doings" only to be told, "Have your mother send her cake."

"Ethel's cake," as it was called, was the recipe of a former neighbor. When Mother, a homesick bride, arrived at the fluorspar mining camp, which was composed of fifty men and no women, her meager cooking skills were no match for the 8,000-foot elevation. A kind rancher's wife rode her horse around the mountain, cake and recipe in hand to welcome her.

Long after we had enjoyed our innocent party, hit the town up for treats, and gone home to bed, store windows were soaped and ash cans dumped. The older and more adventuresome found sport in overturning outhouses. Some of the local men spent hours in their outhouses, doors open, and shot guns loaded with rock salt lying across their knees. Probably more people than just my mother were happy to see Halloween end.

❖ CHRISTMAS ❖

Throughout the war years Christmas remained as former Christmases; but it was scaled back, required more ingenuity and a sense of humor. Getting a tree was a good example. With my father's long workdays he wasn't available to go tree hunting, so Mother announced early one December Sunday that we'd all ride to the mine with him. While Dad worked, Mother, my sister, and I were going to locate, chop down, and carry a tree back to our car. It sounded like a wonderful adventure, a perfect way to get us in the Christmas spirit and a chance to get our tree "up" before anyone else. During the drive we discussed how we'd find the perfect tree. If either of our parents were skeptical they remained silent and didn't spoil the occasion by reminding us that the pines around the mine weren't straight, full and proud, as a Christmas tree should be.

When we arrived we didn't waste any time locating a stand of trees about a mile away, and from a distance they all looked perfect. Off we set, Mother carrying the hatchet and leading the way. She started up the haul road which, while covered with a foot of new snow, made for easier walking than taking off cross-country. We plodded behind her, so she could break trail. We rested often and every few minutes I stopped to see if we were getting closer to the chosen trees. We weren't! It soon became obvious that we'd set our sights too far. Maybe we could find a "good" tree nearby.

As we climbed higher, there were drifts across the road, the wind was colder, and the outing wasn't as much fun as we'd anticipated. We left the road to inspect the trees in the nearby draw. We could tell they weren't as nice as we wanted, but as we sank down through two to three feet of snow, we struggled just to reach those "straggly" few. They definitely weren't worthy of Christmas status, and we insisted on going to the clump above us. We fought our way upward to the next bunch and the next, until I announced I could go no farther.

Mother realized that one of these misfits would have to do. Margaret was disappointed, I no longer cared, and Mother proceeded to chop down the best of the lot. It took her a long time. My feet were wet from where the snow had spilled over my galoshes and sifted into my shoes. I stomped my wet feet to keep them warm. Finally the tree fell forward, and it was apparent that most of its branches were on one side.

We dragged it out of the draw, retracing our steps up the slope to the road. There we rested until the wind forced us to head downward. As we pulled the tree behind us, precious needles and small branches remained in our wake, and by the time we reached the car, the tree was a naked shadow of its former self. Mother assured us it just needed lights and icicles.

When we returned home we leaned it against the wall way in the back corner near the one electrical outlet in the living room. Dad made a stand for it from two short slabs nailed crosswise, and then he drilled a hole in the center. The best side faced the front, which improved its looks, but straightening the trunk was impossible. It was obvious our tree possessed none of the qualities we had sought.

My father laid three strings of colored lights on the floor and plugged them in to see if they would light. If there was one bad bulb along the string, none would light, and there were no available bulbs to buy. After checking out each bulb it took all of the strands that we owned to make one good one. This strand he draped around our homely tree spreading the bulbs as far apart as possible so as to have lights from top to bottom. Then he retreated behind his newspaper and left to Mother the task of placing the top on, a silver and blue star with a point broken off. She also hung a few balls near the top which was too high for us to reach.

Now it was up to my sister and me to complete the task, and we began harmoniously to hang balls and bells from the "scruffy" branches. We put most of the ornaments to the center-front since that was where the limbs were, and we assured ourselves we could fill in the holes with dangling icicles. But there were too many holes, and I got tired of draping each icicle carefully among the remaining needles. I resorted to grabbing a handful and hurling them at the tree with the hope some would "stick." This brought protests from my sister and Mother from the kitchen.

The joyous occasion of "tree getting" ended with tears, me kicking my sister, and getting sent from the room where I sat pouting on a folding chair just around the corner. Peace was finally restored, and a white sheet was bundled around the tree base to resemble snow and to cover the board stand. Dad lowered his paper while we all admired our handiwork. He said, "This is a hard luck tree with lots of character." I took his statement to mean he really liked it.

Mother voiced her opinion saying, "It will be just fine."

I knew it wasn't straight, full, nor proud; but it was still a Christmas tree. And when beneath it I added the cigars I'd bought for my father, the jar of Pond's cream wrapped in red tissue paper for Mother, and the cardboard game with a spinner and cardboard men for my sister, I knew it would be just perfect.

❧ THE FIRE ❦

An early morning fire, fast and cruel, burned the mine mill.

My father ran the fluorspar mine, a collection of old tarpaper and log buildings, shafts, open pits and tunnels. Hidden behind a squatty mountain and above a grassy flat, the mine was tucked into the rocky hillside. It was a place I dearly loved, where I knew every building and every hole in the ground.

On the shelf in the mine office I kept my own hard hat, stuffed with newspaper to fit my head, and beside it a carbide lamp. With the weight of the lamp hooked on the front of the hard hat, I had all I could manage to hold my head up. However I gladly accepted a headache or stiff neck for the chance to go underground. I was very proud of my outfit, and even more proud of being with my father. Whenever possible, I was his shadow. With me trudging behind him, we entered the dark tunnel, trying to avoid the mud created by the perpetual stream of water that flowed between the tracks. When a train of mine cars filled with ore and muck came out, we jumped to one side and pressed against the wooden timbers that supported the tunnel roof. My father often grabbed a chunk of rock from the passing train to check its quality, while I grinned, hoping the miners noticed me.

Fluorspar came from thick veins in the ground and was hauled by truck or mine cars to the mill. The mill, built in 1925, leaned into the hill with tall black walls stalking upward, few windows, and many wooden steps that led to the crushers, pick'n belts, screens, and finally the loadout. The jarring of the crushing rock made a deafening roar, shook the building, and filled the air with a dusty cloud.

On that cold winter morning when the phone rang and we learned the mill was a smoldering ruin, I begged and pleaded to go see what was left. Instead I was sent to school where I expressed my belief that it was obviously sabotage. Sabotage was a very slight possibility; but, until the FBI arrived, nothing was touched and a watchman stood guard. Every evening my father sat at the kitchen table making rough drawings on a tablet.

The following weekend when I finally got to the mine, the twisted metal and burnt timbers took my breath away and brought tears to my eyes. I wandered around on that gray day and finally sat down on an empty dynamite box. Above me my father stood looking at what was left of the mill that he had built nearly twenty years before. He stood there a long time.

Within a week the investigation was over, and guilt was placed on aging, frayed electrical wiring. The miners sifted through the rubble, and from what remained and my father's crude designs, an outdoor mill was built near the main tunnel. It was called the Dishpan, an appropriate name for a collection of junk cobbled together in a circle. Somehow it managed to run. In frequently below-zero weather, the crew worked amidst the pitiful, makeshift mill. They were forced to do manually much of what had been mechanically done before. Tonnage was down, but the mine kept running.

During those long days I rarely saw my father. He left very early and came home after my bedtime. So the family could be all together, our weekends were often spent at the mine. I made the rounds with my father, visited with the men, and stood above the slusher, a long piece of metal pulled by cables to drag the ore over the crusher. From my vantage point, I watched with fascination as the boulders disappeared into the crusher's jaws.

We ate lunch in the office laughing and teasing as we sat on folding chairs around a desk. It didn't matter that our plates were pieces of wax paper or that the room was cold and filled with mine dust. To us it was better than a summer picnic.

In the spring a crew arrived to build a new mill—a bigger, quieter, three-story building. It lacked the character of the old mill, but with newer and larger equipment, this mill was capable of producing more. It was during that more promising time that the brakes on one of the dump trucks failed. At first the truck rolled slowly but by the time it hit the front of our car, it was well on its way.

That evening, my father lumbered home in something that resembled a wooden-sided station wagon crossed with a truck. It jerked, bucked, slipped out of gear, and belched smoke; but, after a fashion, it ran. This creature belonged to the mining company and was used as a "step and fetch it" vehicle on the property. To my embarrassment, it became our means of transportation for many months while the local mechanic hunted for parts to repair our car which never totally recovered. To my delight, when the war ended, we were sold the first new car allocated to our county. The '46 Chevy was the same style and color of the pre-war cars, a greenish gray with 1940 lines; but it looked new, it smelled new, and it was the envy of all my friends.

❧ LNP&W ❧

The train tracks which cut through the mine ranch were indented into the side of Sentinel Mountain. It wasn't a steep mountain and probably wouldn't have been noticed most places; but its location, sprawling out into North Park, made it something of a landmark. Most of the mountain was rock, grass, and sagebrush covered, but there were thick groves of aspens higher up on the north side and pines on the north and east. We looked at the mountain frequently, not because of its prominence, but because we were watching for the train. Father frequently asked, "Any ore cars on the train today?"

The train captivated me. I sat on the porch, my feet wrapped around the legs of the folding chair, sugar spilling off my bread, butter, and sugar sandwich while my eyes searched for the familiar smoke and black engines-there were two needed because of the steep climb. The train wasn't easy to miss. From the time it chugged out of the canyon until it disappeared around the southern reaches of Sentinel it was close to an hour. As it climbed above the hayfields and

Pinkham Creek, it was in sharp contrast to the land-scape. In the evenings I enjoyed seeing the train's shadows flash against the bank as they tried to keep up. I could hear the engines labor, slowly pulling their load on to Walden and further south to Coalmont, where coal-filled cars waited to be hauled back to Laramie and the main Union Pacific line. The LNP&W stood for the Laramie, North Park and Western Railroad. But my sister and I called it the Lazy, No Pep & Wobbly. It wasn't an original saying of ours, and we usually just said "the train." The track, while a little over a hundred miles long, was a branch of the Union Pacific.

The climb from the plains of Wyoming over the top and into Colorado was slow and arduous. There were several switchbacks, and the train crossed the road five or six times as it wended its way southward. It hauled cattle, coal, fluorspar, timber, and at one time people.

My parents came to North Park on the LNP&W in March of 1925, after coming west on the train from St. Louis. Father was Leadville born but had been out of our state for many years. While building a mill in Illinois he met my mother who had never been west of the Mississippi. She was small town, Ohio River raised and a bewildered bride. She told us of looking out the window seeing snow and trees, trees and snow while she searched for people and houses. She had looked forward to this new adventure of a home in a mining camp in the mountains of Colorado. My father was exhilarated by his return to his birth state and the challenge of building another mill.

After a joltingly long ride, the train stopped once more for water, and my father announced to mother that they were almost there. She strained to see some kind of civilization but where there weren't trees, it was all white and she became frightened. Now their journey took them through what appeared to be a tunnel of cold. Inside the jerking car it was almost as dark as night. When the train next stopped, it just stopped! There was no siding, water tower or depot. Waiting alongside the tracks was a man with a sled pulled by a team of horses.

Mother told us often about that first trip. She pointed to a spot not far above my favorite fishing hole. "That is where we got into the sled with our big trunk wedged in behind us. I'd never been on such a sled." The last lap of the trip was a cold two-mile ride around Dean Peak to the small, primitive mining camp. There a two room, chinked log cabin was her new home. Mother said, "My tears almost washed the mountains away."

I knew she was exaggerating. I dreamt of riding the train, but no one rode the train now except the people shipping their cattle. We drove.

Although the train didn't haul passengers, it was the lifeblood of the area. It made three trips a week, taking a day to come into the park and a day to go back outside. Much of our war effort was carried away by the LNP&W.

The fluorspar loadout was close by, and when we went for the mail, we stopped to see how many cars were filled and ready to ship. We watched the trucks back up to the ramp and dump over the side into the cars. My father swung up onto the side of a car where he grabbed a handful of ore, checking its quality. I could never figure out how, with one fistful, he knew if the ore was high grade or just "fair to middling." He even knew if it came from the pit or underground, and what the assay would likely read. It all looked the same to me.

Once in a great while a train came while we were at the loadout. I was thrilled as it backed into the siding and coupled the cars together. We knew some of the trainmen who shouted and waved to us before they slowly chugged away. My father always seemed relieved to be sending the fluorspar off to steel mills and other wartime destinations.

❧ THE FUNERAL ❧

She had been to Mass, fixed breakfast, and packed her son's lunch. Then my eighty-six-year-old grandmother sat down in a living room chair and died. Although this small Irish woman with startling blue eyes and a lingering brogue was my grandmother, she was not well known to me. We rarely saw her. We hadn't had a vacation in three years. Although my father called her when there were open phone circuits, to me she was grandmother in name only.

The call came from Salt Lake City, Utah. It was only four hundred miles from our Colorado home, but the trip posed many problems. How do we get there? We didn't have enough gas coupons to drive. Should my father leave work? The mine had a defense contract to meet. He usually worked six or seven days a week, and, most important, should he go alone?

I stood around waiting to hear what was going to happen and rather looking forward to a possible trip. Then I noticed the tears in my father's eyes, and they gave new meaning to the phone call. I patted his hand as he put shirts in his suitcase, but he paid no attention to my gesture, which surprised me. He seemed so far away. I sat down on the bed where I could keep an eye on him.

A decision in favor of the entire family going was finally made. We drove sixty miles to the nearest train station in Laramie, Wyoming, where we hoped to get on a passenger train. We left as soon as possible; and, except for stopping because I suffered from motion sickness, we had no trouble on the first leg of our journey.

When we arrived at the depot, we soon learned that getting on a train without reservations was unthinkable. The green chalkboard along one wall told of arrivals and departures, but it was ignored because the few passenger trains that stopped in Laramie ran from four to six hours late. So we waited and waited. The high-backed wooden benches were uncomfortable, and running and sliding on the slick, marble floors in the ladies room quickly grew tiresome. My father spent hours at the ticket window pleading our case over and over until finally, toward evening, they sold us tickets and let us board the westbound Portland Rose.

We were now on a train, going the right direction, but had no seats. At the end of one car we found room to stand our suitcases on end and sit down on them. With the swaying and jerking of the train, it took effort and balance for me to keep contact with the suitcase. It was going to be a long night.

Help came in the form of a slightly drunk army private. He was weaving toward the back of the car when he spotted us. The soldier offered his upper berth and said he'd ride in the men's room. My father eagerly agreed to take him up on his offer, promptly paid for the upper berth and joined the private in the men's room. There they spent the night on a narrow bench with the soldier's head resting on my father's shoulder.

My mother, sister, and I crawled up into the bunk where I was pressed against the wall. Margaret occupied the middle third of the bed, and Mother clung to the edge. I didn't like the idea of my father being separated from us. I felt we should be close by just in case he was sad.

Most of the night was spent waiting for troop trains. They had first choice on the railroad tracks, and we spent hours on a siding somewhere in Wyoming. At last there was the rumbling and vibrating as the troop train passed; and, when all was calm, we continued on our way until it happened again in early morning. When we finally chugged into Salt Lake City, it was nearly noon. There we discovered that taxicabs were as scarce as train seats; and, once more, we waited and waited.

The trip wasn't what I'd hoped for, and my grandmother's funeral was something of a shock. Her small brick home filled a narrow lot with a patch of grass out front and a cement porch. The streetcar barns, a block long, loomed across the street. In her tiny living room, with walls weighted down with large family portraits in dull silver frames, was Grandmother.

To my horror, her casket, lid open, had been wedged into the room. I had not counted on Grandmother being so present, nor did I suspect we'd be frequently called upon to cram into the living room to pray for Grandma. The house filled and emptied many times during the next two days as old friends and neighbors stopped in to pay their respects. The mortuary had furnished folding chairs for the crowd and a kneeler for the "prayers."

"Such a shock!" "Such a blessing." "What a wonderful way to go." "Looks just like Maggie." "The O'Donnell Funeral Home always does a good job."

When I wasn't checking on my father, I tried to hide on the wooden back porch, but someone was forever dragging me out to meet a newcomer.

"Aye, and this will be Maggie's granddaughter, one of Mike's girls."

"She has the round face, but where's the red hair?"

At last they took Grandmother to the church. In that roomier place, I sat in a pew, swung my feet back and forth, and whirled a rosary around my wrist until an uncle planted an elbow in my ribs.

Maggie came over from Ireland to the mining town of Leadville, Colorado, where she was hired as a nanny for an Irish judge. She met and married another Irishman who was a miner, a policeman, and my grandfather. Until sometime after 1900, Maggie helped feed their four children by running a boarding house. They moved on to another mining town, Park City, Utah, where Grandma lost a son in a mining accident, and years later she moved to Salt Lake City, Utah. What impressed me most about her was how my grandmother had struggled up the long hill to the small, brick church, every morning for more than thirty years. She never missed mass.

On hearing that I didn't know why it took us three days to bury Grandma. I figured she went from that chair right to heaven and didn't need any help from us. I peeked over at my father, and I think he felt the same way, too.

We had time to see cousins and visit; but, between the company and the visiting, my father was constantly on the phone trying to get reservations for our return trip. After much perseverance he got two upper berths, again on the Portland Rose, and we went home in style.

❧ THE GOOSE ❧

The closest grocery to our summer home, the Cowdrey Store, had two entrances. One was more or less forgotten but it was the original door and was set three or four feet into the two story, white stucco building. It faced south, and at one time the road to Walden passed in front of it. The second door, on the east side and beneath an added-on canopy which covered the gas pumps and faced the new road, was the door of choice.

We usually drove under the canopy, and I was usually the first one out of the car, and usually the first one to the candy counter. If there were any kids within a "holler," when they saw our car drive up, they hustled to the store. My father was always good for a sack of whatever candy was available. I never saw him refuse to shell out a nickel, dime or quarter, whatever it took, to treat the Cowdrey kids.

But there were times when I was last, and there were times when I used the original door, and sometimes I just sat in the car, angry and dejected. It was all because of a goose. Old

Goosey, as we called her, belonged to the store-keeper-postmaster. She waddled around the building, south side to east side and even out back. It all depended on the weather and her mood. No one paid much attention to her-except me. Goosey didn't like me, and I was afraid of her-perhaps terrified was a better word. She came running when she saw me, feet slapping the ground, neck stretched way out and wings flapping. A hoarse honk erupted from her throat. She nipped me more than once. Old Goosey could ruin a perfectly good trip to the store.

I looked forward to the Cowdrey jaunt. The population was less than one hundred, but it was more than a wide spot in the road. The hamlet was the hub for an area that stretched northward about thirteen miles to the Wyoming border, to the Medicine Bow Range to the east, nine miles south to Walden, and westward to the mountains and lakes of the Continental Divide. Its post office, store, and garage served ranchers, loggers, and miners and their families as did the one room, eight-grade school. But besides these necessities, Cowdrey represented a community where friends and neighbors met, business was conducted, and ideas exchanged.

One day when the goose was on the prowl and I was stuck in the car, my father, the store-owner, and a rancher "hunkered down" on the side near the original door. Sitting on their heels, their backs pressing the smooth wall, they held a Republican caucus. There were a couple of folding chairs leaning against the wall for the meeting "goers," but they were ignored, maybe too sissy for the Republicans. They met, war or not, to select delegates for the county convention. Who were they for, and what was their platform? There didn't appear to be many disagreements as they talked, the sun warming the building and in turn warming their backsides.

Smoked drifted around the corner as two of them puffed on fat cigars. It was difficult to hold a meeting as no one could really spare the time, but all agreed that the democratic process was one of the freedoms the war was all about.

The 1944 election starred Franklin Delano Roosevelt who was running for his fourth term as president. He'd been the headman since before I was born and while I found Delano a strange name, I thought the Republicans' choice, Thomas Dewey, had a mustache that too closely resembled the enemy's. The Democrats' campaign slogan that stated America should not "change horses mid-stream" conjured up pictures of cowboys leaping from horse to horse in the middle of the Platte River—something I would have loved to have witnessed.

So they met, talked, and wrote on the back of an envelope, frequently interrupted by someone who wanted a stamp, hunk of baloney, or gallon of kerosene. All the while I sat trapped. Goosey strutted around the car, her two black, penetrating eyes watching for any movement from within. There was no escape until the meeting ended, the mail was gathered, and we drove the five miles home.

❧ THE READING ❧

One of my most unpleasant memories occurred when I gave my first and last "reading." It all began when the teacher stopped me in the hallway. "I want you to give a reading for the Woman's Club next Tuesday."

"Do what?"

"Someone called and the ladies want a reading for the program part of their meeting. Please stay after school." And off she went while I lamented the dismal fact that I had to remain longer than I liked in the white, stucco cube which reminded me more of a marshmallow than a school.

We were a long way from a city so everyone did their part to make our community seem less remote; and, while culture wasn't a buzz-word then, we did strive for some of the finer things of life.

I stayed as told, and the teacher dragged out a worn-looking booklet titled *The Kaffeeklatsch*. It was about three Swedish ladies having coffee. As I remember one of the women did most of the talking and she was quite a gossip.

I dutifully went over the reading and struggled to sound like a Swede. The teacher wasn't much help, even though she said she was part Swedish. I understood her problem for she had been away to college; and, besides that, English teachers are supposed to sound like, well, English teachers.

Now our county was full of Swedish ranchers, and many had come from the old country. On the other hand, I'm mostly Irish and I hadn't paid much attention to the speech of all those people whose names ended in "son." For all I knew we all sounded just the same.

My mother listened as I stumbled through *The Kaffeeklatsch* and, in desperation, suggested I wear something appropriate for a klatsch. She must have called some older women because my borrowed outfit turned out to be old and smelled of mothballs. The garb consisted of a navy blue crepe dress that hung about ankle length. The sleeves were long and rather full while the large square collar, made of starched white lace, hung almost to my waist. Below were my brown Girl Scout shoes with arch supports and white anklets. This ridiculous outfit was topped with a blue felt hat. The creation had a small brim over which spilled a gathered black veil that ended mid-forehead. The rest of the hat, a circle of gathered net and felt, perched on my head like a bird's nest.

I was worried about the "reading," but I was more worried my friends might see me in the klatsch costume, and I was most worried about my mother. Several days before the club meeting Mother developed rheumatism. As long as I can remember, my mother lumped all her ailments into one category—rheumatism.

If ever I needed her support from the folding chairs it was this time, and she was sick. The pain located in her shoulder was treated with aspirin and, for added relief, she tied a tea towel around her neck as a sling. Hot toddies were my father's treatment for most ailments. He made her one with his Irish whiskey. That toddy sent her reeling to the couch, still clutching her shoulder. With the nearest doctor sixty-three miles away, Mother was chained to her rheumatism, and I was doomed to perform alone.

I got home from school on the meeting Tuesday, put on the klatsch outfit, and practiced "the reading" one final time. At the last minute, Mother added some horn-rimmed glasses with the lenses missing to the costume and I ran up the street to the community church, home of the

Woman's Club. There, in a circle on the folding chairs, sat my audience.

The "reading" I have managed to blot from my memory, but the twenty or thirty minutes that followed I can't forget. I knew I had failed when two Swedish ladies took me aside and attempted to give me a lesson in talking "Swede." Others questioned my Kaffeeklatsch outfit. "Where had it come from?" And everyone asked, "Where is your mother?"

Afterwards I raced home, not even staying for refreshments, with the hat bouncing on my head and the glasses sliding down my nose, while tears softened the starched lace collar. I was prepared to burst into the house and fall sobbing into my mother's arms, but when I saw her through the window trying to cook and hold a hot water bottle to her shoulder, I dried my eyes on the long, blue sleeve and reported, "I did OK."

I've often wondered if she ever heard the truth. I know I never told her, and I never told her that I vowed that Tuesday afternoon that I'd never give another reading. She might have been relieved.

❧ SPRING ❧

May had three joyous occasions for me: May Basket Day, the school picnic, and the last day of school. These were minor holidays to most people; but to one who didn't enjoy school, loved picnics and relished the anticipation of giving a May basket without getting caught, they were important dates.

As I trod the well-worn path around sagebrush, through back yards, and along fences up the hill to school, the signs of spring appeared. Of all the omens, such as disappearing snow banks and drying mud holes, the most exciting was the appearances of tiny buttercups, a bright waxy yellow flower, and the taller, indigo bluebell. I greeted these harbingers of spring and the coming freedom like good friends from the past. Not only did these wild flowers herald the season but I picked them for my mother and May baskets.

When constructing my May baskets, I preferred the cone shaped ones, mainly because they were easy to make. I'd mix up a batch of paste from flour and water, then roll a half sheet of construction paper so it was narrow on one end and wider on the other to hold the chosen goodies. I used lots of paste, and it often leaked out leaving ugly, white, rough globs around the seam. The same thing happened when I added a paper handle, but all in all, the six or eight I made for my friends didn't look too bad, especially when filled with cookies or candy and the flowers.

The tough part was sneaking up to the friend's house, hanging the basket on the door knob, knocking and running away before I got caught, which meant I got kissed. Since my basket handles were weak, I learned to lean the creation against the door and then tear around the corner where I could peak at the surprised "receiver." After delivering one or two, I raced home to sit on a folding chair right inside our door to await a "basket delivery." I was a slow runner so even with my close presence to the "knocker," I rarely caught anyone.

The school picnic just before the final day usually involved some parents and younger brothers and sisters. Since we had no school buses, we either walked or jammed into a few cars. If it was a walking affair, we carried a sack lunch, and some of us took along a fishing pole.

A favorite spot, but too far to walk to, was the sand hills. The clean, white sand, blown against the mountains, formed high dunes dotted along the edges with a few hardy trees. Whether we were digging tunnels or playing a slow motion game of softball, the picnic was, without fail, a huge success.

However I always secretly hoped the teacher would pick "the teepees," a rocky area north of town where nature had left big, rounded boulders, piled on each other and interspersed with paths and pines. This had been a campsite for early Ute Indians, evident by teepee rings, raised poles and fire pits. The Utes had hunted the area for many years, camping in this protected place where there was water close by and bountiful game. In the shadow of our county's history we hid from each other, climbed on the rocks, and explored the paths.

The "teepees" was not a first choice of the parents however, as they worried about falls from the rocks, but of more concern, "the teepees" had a surplus of wood ticks. Spring brought out these persistent, tenacious bugs. As soon as we got home, Mother did a shake down. She checked behind our ears, in our hairlines and from there on down to our toes. With luck, if any were found they were still moving and easily removed. If they were stuck with their heads buried into our skin it was time to howl, "Don't burn me!" A match was struck and held close to the bug. When the tick got too warm, it backed out to free itself. My fear was always that I would get too warm first.

About three weeks after May Day, I celebrated the last day of school. It was low key but I could almost feel the shackles fall away as I cleaned out my desk. There were papers shoved to the back, probably those that had messages from the teacher saying the assignment was messy or full of "poor spelling." There were notes, pencil stubs, and a long missing eraser.

We took turns taking down the sun-faded artwork from the walls and passing it out. Next came the folders that held our book reports (mine was thinner than most), the long narrow spelling tests with a few stars for perfect papers, and finally those exceptional papers the teacher just couldn't part with until the end of the year. She seemed to love a few of my arithmetic tests.

The teacher had a few last minute instructions such as taking home any left-over clothing articles that were hanging on the pegs outside the classroom door. She urged us to read *Our Weekly Reader,* a four-page newspaper that we had ordered earlier. I thought it was dull but knew I'd read it as my mother wasn't about to waste the fifty-cent subscription.

The teacher read stories until the bell rang, then we grabbed our papers, said a polite, "Have a nice summer," and rushed outside. We drank in the cool May air as we chanted, "School's out, school's out! The teacher let the monkeys out!"

May not only welcomed spring but also meant a summer move to the ranch and three months of freedom.

HOW COULD
❧ THIS HAPPEN? ❧

How could this happen in our little town? I watched the movie newsreels, read, and heard on daily radio broadcasts about people being killed. Our American servicemen were dying all over the globe. People suffered through the nightly bombings in England, and planes were being shot down over France, Germany and the Pacific Ocean, but nothing affected me like the death of my friend's mother.

How could she do that? I didn't want to believe that a mother died. War hadn't killed her, she died of a brain hemorrhage. I was there but I didn't know what was going on—it happened so fast.

Shuffling home one Saturday, I was thinking more about lunch possibilities than the familiar car that stopped out in the middle of the street. The door opened but no one got out. I saw a woman slump onto the seat. What had she dropped on the car floor? I started across the street, but a pickup stopped alongside so I ambled home. Nothing ever happened on main street, and besides people often stopped to visit, give a message, or whatever. Stopping in the street never caused a traffic jam. Nothing bad ever happened, especially to a mother.

"Would you like to go to the funeral with me?" my mother asked.

"No, no." I didn't want to go, I couldn't go, and I wouldn't go. I didn't know how I'd ever face my friend. What would I say? "No, I'll stay home," I said.

But instead of staying home, I wandered down the street and followed the road out of town. I climbed through a barb wire fence onto the field of a rancher. He never minded the kids crossing his field to fish in the river and, besides, he was probably at the funeral.

I didn't go any farther than the haystack in the middle of the field where I crawled through the stack fence and sat down on the south side. The sun was warm and I was protected from the wind. Our town topped the gentle hill before me, but the church was hidden from view by homes and trees. I leaned against the hay even though it poked and scratched my back. I settled in for the afternoon, but something was wrong. I didn't like what I was thinking, "traitor, coward," or words to that effect. I should have gone to the funeral. I should have been there for my friend. I should have asked my mother if she was feeling well.

"Dear Lord, don't you dare take my mother away."

I didn't last long by the haystack, and soon I was back in town where I hung over the picket fence across the street from the church. There were cars parked everywhere, more cars than came to the parade. Where did they put everyone? It wasn't long before I found out.

The church double doors opened, and I could see people sitting on the steps inside. There were folding chairs in the vestibule and men leaning against the wall. They slowly came out onto the walk where they formed a tunnel for the rest to walk through. Some nodded to others or briefly shook hands, but no one visited.

It was a long time before my mother came out, and I was relieved to see her take a place on the lawn. She had probably gotten there early and had a good seat up front. She stood with her hands folded before her, her purse hanging from her wrist. She was wearing that awful brown crepe dress that I just hated. It made her look old. Old!

"Dear Lord, let my mother live a long time."

Then I heard sobbing and out came the family, clinging to one another. My friend leaned on her older sister looking small, lost, and so alone.

I felt my own tears dripping onto my shirt. I was thankful when my mother saw me and came across the street. She put her arm around me and we stood together until the procession had gone to the cemetery. Car after car followed the big, black hearse which had come from Laramie. The Town Marshal's car was in the lead to stop any approaching traffic, but there was no traffic to stop as everyone in town was following him.

The cemetery was just a block away on the bluff of a hill with a wire fence around it and fences around some of the graves. There was very little grass, mostly sagebrush, dirt, and rocks. Mother usually joined those who walked, but this time we started home. We walked silently to the end of the short sidewalk, then in the dirt street in front of the postmaster's house, and into our driveway.

"You'll have lots of chances to be a good friend," she said.

I nodded and gulped and sniffled. How could this happen? Mothers don't die.

❧ Graduation ❧

The highlight of every spring, one to be anticipated from April on, was the high school graduation. It didn't matter if the graduates were relatives, friends, or neighbors-everyone knew everyone else. So whether it was six, sixteen or a rare twenty graduates, we all turned out and filled the dark, box-like gymnasium to salute our graduates, especially those going into the armed services.

Every year, I looked forward to the commencement and got to the high school early where I hurried down the eight or ten concrete steps to the garden level gym to get first pick of the folding chairs. I didn't want a front row seat but rather a center aisle one about half way back. With luck my friend Shirley would arrive shortly after I did, and together we eagerly awaited the piano rendition of "Pomp and Circumstance." The old upright piano was rolled out of the corner of the boys' locker room and shoved against the wall beneath the stage.

The gym filled and, with the opening chords, our excitement mounted until we could hardly contain our giggles as the "lame duck" procession began. From the back came the graduates: step, feet together, pause, and step forward with the other foot. Our eyes were glued on the feet, or to be more precise, the ankles of the girls. We cared nothing about the purple mortarboards with their gold tassels and matching robes.

For most of the girls, graduation meant getting their first pair of high heels and, while making it to the stage would have been difficult for a "high-heeled" walking pro, it was a killer for amateurs. Step, and one ankle trembled, pause, and the other quaked. We loved it and leaned out of our chairs to watch as those shaky ankles wobbled and rolled their way past the crowd and mounted the four steep, narrow steps of the temporary staircase leading to the center of the stage. Inexperienced ankles were no match for the rail-less steps. More than a few girls mounted those stairs with terror on their faces and arms flailing, the dark purple sleeves flapping, like distressed tightrope walkers. When they had conquered the steps and made their way to the places of honor, their relief was obvious.

For Shirley and me, it was better than an Abbott and Costello movie, and when the procession was over, we sank back in our chairs, weak from stifling our giggles. We settled down for the prayer, boring speeches, a song or two, and finally the passing out of the diplomas. Then once more we sat up, alert and ready to laugh again.

At the east end of our dinky gym, with its chicken-wire covered ceiling to protect the lights, was the stage. Swaddled in a gray material around the sides and back, it was framed with royal purple velvet curtains. Across the top hung the same heavy velvet in a draped fashion and adorned with long gold fringe. I thought it had a regal look.

At the appointed time, the president of the school board, a giant of a man, rose from his seat at the back of the stage. This rancher, who always wore cowboy boots adding several more inches to his height, had been on the school board for so many years that we knew exactly what he'd say and do. We loved it. As he walked to the podium, he appeared to be a man without a head because the purple drape and gold fringe cut his head off from the audience's view.

From what we thought was a hilarious position, the headless president called out the names while we poked each other in the ribs. It was a repeat of the shaky ankles with the added attraction of the missing head. We dutifully withheld our applause until all the diplomas were dispensed. Then the rancher bent down and leaned way out from the stage until his head appeared in front of the purple and the gold.

"Let's give our graduates a big hand," his voice boomed.

The gym resounded with our clapping until the head disappeared again. The graduation was over. The music began, but there wasn't much of a recessional as the well-wishers pushed forward, filling the aisle, and reaching up to shake hands.

Years later I should have paid for my enjoyment of the graduates' misery, but I was spared. Two years before I graduated, a new gymnasium was built with a "hidden-from-view," permanent stairway and railing leading to the stage. No one saw my ankles, and besides from years of observation, I knew enough to buy my heels early and practice, practice, practice.

❧ LIVING OFF THE LAND ❧

"Victory Garden? In this country? It can freeze any day of the year." That was my mother's reply to my idea that we grow our own vegetables. All were urged to raise as much of their own produce as possible, but that was one patriotic war effort we never undertook. A Victory Garden was out of the question.

There were shortages from time to time and not a lot of variety, but we never went hungry. If a peddler came by, we had fresh fruit and vegetables for several days and peaches to can. My sister and I sat in the big kitchen and peeled. We each had a paring knife and an enamel pan in our laps. Mother dipped a strainer full of peaches into the kettle of boiling water, just long enough to loosen the skins, and then scooped six or eight peaches into our bowls to halve, pit and slip the skin off. Usually there was a contest going on to see who could "peel" the perfect peach. From there the halves went into a kettle of cold water with a little vinegar added to keep them from darkening. A full kettle of peaches meant a break for us while mother cooked them, gently spooned them into sterilized jars, covered each quart with hot syrup, and sealed them.

The sweet smell from the kettles steaming on the black coal stove, the breeze coming in through the screen door, and the juicy taste of a stolen peach half made canning a pleasant, rewarding time.

But there were summers when the peddlers didn't come. Then with no peddlers or Victory Gardens, we looked for what grew close to home. Some years the wild gooseberries were plentiful, and a tart pinkish and green gooseberry pie was grand. When word got around that there were ripe berries in the willows along the creek, we organized an expedition. Usually eight or ten of us met and hiked together to the site that supposedly had the most gooseberries. Walking through the pasture, kicking up the September layer of dust, was one of my most favorite times. The gathered women and kids talked, teased, and laughed all the way to the selected patch. That was where the fun ended for me.

Nothing wants to do bodily harm like a goose-berry bush. The wild plant grew toward the center of the thick willows, and it was a chore just to part the willow sticks and wiggle inward where the enemy lay in wait. For every berry, there were two or three thorns, and these needles of pain did everything they could to protect their pea-sized fruit.

We each had a pail with the mothers and older girls carrying large, sturdy buckets. I carried a lighter weight, smaller pail with a shorter handle and "LARD" printed on the side. I stuck my arm through the bail and used it as a shield as I invaded the willows. Once I was situated and as comfortable as I could be with the bramble knives sticking through my pants and shirt, I slipped the pail down my arm until it cradled in my elbow. Then I carefully extended two fingers, latched onto a berry, drew my hand slowly backward and released the round treasure over my pail.

Despairing sounds rose to my ears, as one by one, the berries hit the metal bottom of the bucket. Such hollow sounds. To me they sang out, "You'll never get enough for a pie."

The chatter continued among the pickers, but I was usually quiet as I concentrated on avoiding as many berry-swords as possible. Periodically I let everyone know I was bleeding, but obviously it was each person for herself because I received no sympathy.

When my spot was "picked out," I struggled free and searched for another "berry-loaded" willow. That was always when my mother called out, "Keep picking."

In spite of all the flinches and ouches the smell of damp grass, the sharp flavor of a berry and the sound of a trout jumping in the hidden creek close by created a peaceful setting. My imagination soared. I was Tarzan, hiding in the jungle. Lost in my dreams, I was interrupted by, "Keep picking."

When there was a consensus among the adults that they had enough for pies or batches of jelly, we left the shade and the shadows of the willows. Then my berries shrank before my eyes as we compared our pickings. I poured my gooseberries into my mother's well filled bucket and we retraced our steps through the field.

Now I was free to play, but the pie ordeal had just begun for my mother. After sorting and washing, each tiny stem was plucked from the berries before they were sugared, thickened with flour, and placed into a pie shell to bake.

The day was always a success. We'd seen friends and conquered the gooseberries, but the prize was later when my weary mother drug the card table and folding chairs to the front porch. There in the evening's glow I pointed out to my father the route of the day's journey and related all the pitfalls. Mother presented her work-of-art, a golden latticed pie with those hard-earned berries peeking out.

And my father always said, with a sense of wonder, "Gooseberry pie, my favorite."

CHOKECHERRIES
⇸ AND APRICOTS ⇷

Chokecherries and apricots, two edibles as different as thistles and columbines, were dear to my father's heart and stomach. I'm not quite sure which was his favorite, but I had trouble understanding how something as small, hard, and bitter as a chokecherry could compete with the larger, softer, sweet apricot. Both went back in history to his teenage years.

In the early 1900s, when mining and the town of Leadville faltered, my grandfather grew restless and moved his family—a wife, three sons and a daughter—to Park City, Utah. Once again Grandfather took a job as a miner and rented a wood frame house stuck with other similar homes up a steep hillside where they perched precariously alongside a deep gulch. This house like all its neighbors had a clothes line that was operated from a pulley attached to the back porch and a distant pole across the expanse. It resembled a circus high wire. The pulley reeled the clothes out until they had dried while floating over the deep ravine, and them reeled them back to the house.

My father, an industrious if impatient young fellow of fourteen, landed the job of carrying the mail from Heber City to Park City, some fifteen to twenty miles apart. While riding a horse, an animal he never trusted, with leather mail bags hanging down behind the saddle, he made his way up and down the canyons. Alongside and draped over the trail were chokecherry bushes, some as tall as trees. In late summer they bore clumps of dark purple berries, the size of a cranberry. He would strip a handful from the overhead branches and work them around in his mouth until he got as much of the tart juice as possible. Since there were more seeds than juice it was not a stomach-filling endeavor but rather a love of the peculiar taste.

During those years peddlers from the Provo area and farther south brought wagon loads of their fruits and vegetables to the mountain towns. Besides boxes of bing cherries, they carried ripe apricots, an immediate favorite with my father.

Years later my mother bought sacks of apricots when they were in the stores or from a rare peddler, but the season was short. Once more her rancher friend gave her a winning recipe that prolonged the apricot. Simply called apricot jam, it was more of a conserve with bits of oranges, lemons and pineapple cooked in to produce a thick lumpy spread. We all hovered in the kitchen enjoying the aroma as mother stirred the steaming kettle with a long wooden-handled spatula until the ingredients had combined and thickened into what my father considered to be liquid gold. After pouring the jam into glass jars, Mother sealed them with melted wax. A bowlful was set aside for immediate tasting and, with a little luck, homemade bread or biscuits were available.

North Park also had chokecherry bushes, not as tall or lush as those in Utah, and even when they didn't freeze they produced a much smaller berry. If my father stumbled onto a cluster of ripe ones, he rushed home to announce we were having a picnic supper at the Point of Rocks, a pile of boulders above the Platte River, about three miles from home. Nestled among the rocks were protected chokecherry bushes and a perfect place to play and picnic.

It didn't matter that the prepared supper included mashed potatoes and gravy; Father insisted, to my sister's and my delight, that we have a picnic. Mother folded thick towels around the bowl of potatoes, poured the gravy into a quart jar which she wrapped in newspapers, and off we went.

As soon as we'd consumed the not quite hot supper, we fanned out to pick. We had our usual pails but Father put his berries into his felt hat. He didn't contribute many "pickings" as he put more into his mouth than in his hat. When it got too dark to pick we went home, and as with the apricots, Mother used another pioneer recipe to make chokecherry jelly.

Again from the kitchen wafted a delectable smell. For some strange reason, the boiling chokecherries had a wonderful aroma, far different from their "puckery" taste. Before she began, Mother spread newspapers everywhere because the deep reddish-blue juice stained anything it touched. She poured the juice and berries through a colander to remove the seeds, and then strained it again through cheesecloth.

Now it was ready to boil again, add the pectin, the rationed sugar, and fresh lemon juice. Chokecherry jelly didn't "set up" easily, and it took a practiced eye and constant vigilance to know when it was ready. Over and over Mother dipped the spoon into the boiling brew, catching a small amount and tilting the spoon to let it slide back into the pot. If the syrup sheeted the spoon, it was time to put it into the jelly glasses and top them off with paraffin. In many ways chokecherry jelly was more versatile than apricot jam. Small dishes of the tangy jelly accompanied turkey, ham and baked chicken.

The finished products were lined up on the linoleum-topped counter to be admired before being stored on a cool shelf in the basement. I drew a folding chair close to the cupboard, where I sat counting, rearranging and marveling at each treasure. Before the war was over I too learned to fondly suck on a few berries, spit out the seeds and swallow their bitter juice.

✣ THE FACES OF WAR ✣

On a hot August day, a few weeks before school started, we undertook another Denver trip for the sake of school clothes, a winter coat, and sturdy lace-up shoes. Only this time my father put us on the train in Laramie and returned to the mine. He had pressing work to do, and we were on our own.

The train car was old with red plush seats faded into stripes where the sun had found its way through the slits in the shades. Most of the shades were now stuck in the rolled-up position, and no amount of tugging got them loose. The sun and heat were relentless as we sat on a siding, still in Wyoming and hours from Denver.

Across the aisle was a young couple with a baby not more than two months old. Stashed at their feet was a long, deep, wooden box, obviously homemade. It was something like a trunk except it was painted gray with two black hinges to hold the top on and a catch to keep it shut. The hasp was like the one on our coal shed only it didn't have a padlock on it.

It seemed like every few minutes the woman lifted the lid. Inside, in neat piles, lay diapers and tiny undershirts. There were no little pink dresses or powder blue pants, so I didn't know if the baby was a boy or girl. There was a folded army outfit at one end of the box with polished black shoes tucked alongside.

They sat quietly and the baby was as silent as his or her parents. Except for drinking bottle after bottle of milk that appeared mysteriously from the box and getting jostled a little as the mother tried to change the baby on her lap, the baby slept. In just a diaper and shirt, it was easy to see the thin legs with two inch reddish block-shaped feet attached. I wondered if all new babies looked so starved.

I was sure they were the poorest people I'd ever seen. The woman wore a dull looking flowered dress, scuffed shoes and no stockings. Not having stockings didn't account for much. Silk hose were hard to find as all the silk was going into parachutes. Although I don't know why, even her hair made me think that she was hard up. It was parted in the middle and held behind her ears by two bobby pins.

It was plain to see the man was very young. He had freckles and the usual short military haircut. He never looked at the woman or the baby on her arm, but kept his face turned toward the window. He seemed to swallow a lot.

I put my head down on the back of the seat in front of me and closed my eyes. I didn't want to look at the couple or their baby. They made me sad, and I wished they'd talk or laugh or smile. I suppose they were miserable like everyone else as we waited and waited. I longed to complain that I was too warm, thirsty and tired of waiting in the sun, but I was afraid to be the first to disturb the quiet. My mother was behind me reading *The Denver Post* while my sister, beside me, had her nose buried in a book. Seemed like everyone was dozing or reading except the couple and me.

Finally the door at the other end of the car opened, and a soldier with his coat unbuttoned and his tie loosened walked down the aisle. If he was looking for a cool place, he wouldn't find it here, but at least he made some noise before going through the door at the other end and continuing on his way.

At long last a troop train rushed passed us blotting out the sun for a moment and stirring those sleeping. Minutes passed and still we waited. Why weren't we moving? I wanted to cry. Now our hot car, with its stale air, filled with an even more somber mood, and I blamed it all on the couple and the unrelenting sun.

After what seemed like another hour our train shook again and a second troop train roared by the window. I was glad to know we weren't forgotten or broken down. Slowly we jerked forward. I wanted to cheer, but no one else seemed as elated.

I glanced again at the couple. Even the trains hadn't disturbed the baby as the mother and father kept their lonely sentinel. The woman raised her hand to push aside a damp strand of hair that escaped the bobby pin. She wore a thin gold band on her ring finger, and I couldn't help but notice that she chewed her fingernails. She looked too young to be a mother.

It was mid-afternoon and we should have been in Denver by now. My thoughts turned to how hungry I was and where we'd have supper. If we didn't find a taxicab, we had the options of walking the ten blocks to the hotel or lugging our suitcase onto a street car—not an easy thing to do. While I was contemplating our dilemma the conductor entered the car and began working his way through. Someone asked, "How long before we get to Denver?" Another asked, "How long is the layover?" The conductor's answers were vague, and I decided he didn't know any more than the rest of us. He tried to be cheerful; but his forehead was wet, his collar soaked and he continually wiped his eyes with a big handkerchief.

When he got alongside the couple he seemed to sense their unhappiness and said brightly, "Denver's your destination; I'll give you a hand with your . . ." he glanced down at the box and finally added, "luggage." He seemed a little embarrassed. "Is Denver your home?"

"My folks are there," the woman said softly. "He's shipping out."

I was sure the conductor had heard that before. He just nodded and moved on. "Good luck, son," he said over his shoulder.

As I was eavesdropping, Mother reached around the arm of the chair with a couple of lemon drops for my sister and me. It wasn't much but it would keep me from starving.

When we arrived in Denver we were some of the first off of the train and into the cool cavern of the depot with its stories-high ceiling and amplified echoes. The throng that milled about was like a thousand wind-up toys going this way and that, but not really going anywhere.

Mother hurried us through Denver Union Station as fast as she could, but there were many obstacles as others tried to hustle too. She parked us beside the newspaper stand where a woman sat on a folding chair guarding her papers and metal change box. She eyed us suspiciously. I was relieved to hear Mother's, "Yoo-hoo" and see her waving for us to join her.

We drug the suitcase over to her and hurried to the waiting taxi. As we pulled away from the curb I spied the couple and their baby. They were at the edge of the sidewalk, sitting on their box. I was sure they were waiting again. I was sorry I saw them; it was an image I never forgot.

❧ ANYONE ON THE LINE? ❧

While transportation, coupons, and everyday necessities always created problems, when we moved to the mine ranch in the summer, the telephone proved a nightmare. We were at the end of a party line that went from stubby poles to fence posts and even to the tops of the sagebrush. From time to time, we stopped alongside the road while Dad tried to raise the line off the ground or straighten a tired pole. It was so bad that when he had spent an hour trying to reach the operator, he doubled up his fist and punched the side of the telephone.

For most purposes the phone, a wooden box with a round black mouthpiece attached to the front and accompanied by a cord to the black cylinder to hold to the ear, remained useless. It hung high on the pink kitchen wall behind the round oak table, and I had to stand on a chair to reach the mouthpiece.

Our assigned ring, composed of one long burst and five short ones, was impossible to decipher, so if the phone jingled for a long time, we usually answered by shouting, "Hello, hello, hello, anybody on the line?"

To reach the operator or call the neighbors meant turning the crank on the side of the box. One long ring was the code to reach the operator, and frequently after a vigorous turn someone would come on saying, "I heard a faint ring. Are you trying to reach the operator? I'll ring through for you."

It seemed the farther away from the telephone office, the harder it was to call the operator, and we lived at the end of the phone line.

If Mother was out of the kitchen and the phone rang, even if I knew it wasn't for us, I'd answer it. I always hoped someone would visit for a minute or two, but rarely did anyone have the time. I even tried eavesdropping once when no one was in the house. I heard the ring, climbed up on the chair and carefully lifted up the receiver while I put my other hand over the mouthpiece. The conversation was about cows on the highway. It wasn't worth the sting of the pancake turner across the backs of my legs, and a little farther up, when I got caught.

Some calls were more important than others. If the call was urgent, everyone went about five miles away to the country store, which had two phones. One like ours hung on the wall, right near the mailboxes. It was the same phone line, but closer to the operator. The other phone was in a tall, three-foot by three-foot plywood box with a window on the door. Inside, on a better line, the phoning person felt he had privacy, plus he didn't have to shout. But because it was a flimsy box, those playing cribbage, or just sitting on the folding chairs in the corner, heard every word. From my experience, those calls weren't any more exciting than the ones on our line.

If someone really wanted to get in touch with us, the person gave a note to a miner. He stopped by on his way to work and left it in a wooden box nailed to a post out front. That same box held the two quarts of milk a miner from town dropped off twice a week.

One time, while my father was trying to make a call, several people answered along the line, and in the course of being friendly, Dad asked if there was any news. Someone shouted through the pops and crackles that a prominent rancher in the community had died of a heart attack. At least that was what my father heard, so he passed the sad news along only to learn later that the man was still alive.

"What am I going to do, Ethel?" he asked. "The guy's alive and I can't call anyone on this phone to correct my error." He was as red faced as only an Irishman can get.

Another time, in desperation to get a message to town, my father waved down the bread truck bringing fresh bread to our community from Wyoming. The driver was happy to help out and took the note that read, "Station Agent, we need more ore cars." The bread man dropped it off at the post office and the postmaster put it in the Union Pacific box. It didn't even have a stamp on it, but not long after that empty railroad cars arrived at the train siding where the mine had a loadout chute.

During the last months of the war, our phone rarely even managed a faint tinkle. We were so tired of the communication battle, we surrendered and never turned the "phone crank" again.

⇜ The Sagebrush Heist ⇝

One early summer day we had some excitement in our community. Our post office was robbed. The exact details of the robbery escape me; but I seem to remember that the back door of the post office was forced open, and the villain absconded with both money and mail. I don't know if the robber was apprehended, but the event held a special meaning for me. We all watched for the mail truck that came from Wyoming six days a week. Next to talking about the war or the weather, asking if anyone had seen the mail truck was the most common topic.

Every year or so my mother sent a box of sagebrush to an old friend of hers in southern Illinois. The woman had come to visit before I was born and, for some reason I'll never fathom, she became fond of sagebrush and its "sagey" smell—so fond that she enjoyed having a bouquet in her home.

I grew up thinking sagebrush was about the ugliest, most useless plant that ever existed. It scratched my legs, grew everywhere, was known to house wood ticks and was about as far from green grass and trees as you could get. I always believed that if we had less sagebrush, we'd have more wild flowers and other pretty things.

Never mind what I thought, we went sage-brush gathering with Mother who, armed with a big kitchen knife and a paper sack, led us up the hill before the house. It should have been easy to get a sack full of sagebrush, what with it everywhere, but Mother was picky. She didn't want the thick, twisted, gray plants that grew waist high. We searched for young, smaller shoots that had a slight hint of green to them. If the friend planned to put it in a vase, the older stuff would never do. For my part, I'd have been ashamed to have that sack of brush displayed in our home. People would have thought we'd gone crazy and probably would have complained about its awful smell.

As our trek progressed, we trudged along the hillside and wandered down into the flat that led to the mine. When my mother found a plant she liked she sawed away on its trunk with her knife, even though it was hard on both Mother and the knife for even young sagebrush is as tough as range rope. Then she sniffed it, and if it had the right "sagey" smell, I held open the sack and the sagebrush was placed with care inside. This search, saw, and smell routine went on for an hour or two.

I added to the occasion by complaining, "I'm hot, I'm thirsty, my feet hurt. When are we going home?"

After gathering the sagebrush, Mother wrapped it loosely in newspaper, put it in a box and when we went to town, it got mailed. It just so happened it got mailed the day the post office was robbed. What a shock to our community! Stealing mail was unthinkable.

After hearing the news, I imagined the thief sneaking the box from the post office, throwing it into his get-away car, and racing off. He probably hadn't gone far when he began to smell the strong sagebrush odor. It might have made him sick, so sick he had thrown the package from the window. I preferred to think he stopped at a deserted cabin where he sat on a folding chair out front and went through his loot, tearing apart letters and boxes. I could just see the look on his face when he opened up the sagebrush.

I never heard if the stolen mail was recovered. But it took more than a thief to deter my mother, and it wasn't long after the robbery that we climbed the hill—back on another sagebrush expedition.

❧ ENTERTAINMENT ❧

When haying season arrived in late July or early August, our country's shortage of workers was apparent. The few hay hands that rode the bus into North Park seeking employment were usually too sick, too old, or too drunk to work. The ranchers who met the bus looking for help often went home disappointed, while many young friends about our age went into the fields to harvest the hay.

Mostly they raked, driving an old team that knew the art of haying better than their driver. The animals had no intention of running away.

I thought it looked like a glamorous job and suggested to my folks that I wanted to be a raker. Not only was I totally inexperienced, but I also had hay fever. Throughout the summer I spent most of my time blowing my nose on one of my father's white handkerchiefs and sucking on half a lemon. I was easy to spot at a distance what with the white flag always before my face.

Instead of a haying career I spent most of my summer looking for fun things to do. With my sister and our friend, who also lived on the ranch, we played cowboys and Indians. There were two bicycles among the three of us, and the bikes represented the horses. The Indian was always my role, and since I was the youngest and most gullible, I fell for all the ploys. Frequently I was told to go lie by the trail. Evidently I was an injured Indian, and the cowboys would save me. I wonder how many hours I stretched out beneath the sagebrush waiting to be rescued. If there was an anthill nearby, I contended with ants crawling on me while the bikes whizzed by. After awhile I got up, brushed off the dirt and ants and tattled to Mother. Occasionally I was spared when we were called upon to take a cold drink to those working in the fields.

Compared to being the "horseless" Indian, walking on stilts was a better choice of entertainment for me, for we each had a pair. Mine were about ten inches off the ground, my sister's a foot or so, and our friend, the oldest, rode her's close to two feet off the ground. A man that worked at the mine made them for my father. They were constructed from scrap two-by-fours, and the straps to hold our feet in place were strips of old conveyor belt. By taking small steps and holding on tightly to the top of the stilts, we were able to go anywhere.

One danger area for stilt walkers was the slough and bogs beside our well. I tried to keep up by taking a short cut through that swamp, and it never failed that I got a stilt stuck in the black mire. As the stilt sank, an ominous sucking sound rose from the goo. I fought desperately to plant the other stilt on solid ground. After pumping the free stilt up and down, I tilted backwards, to the sides, and then over I pitched. Knees, shoes, hands, and arms lathered in slimy mud.

It was the perfect time to wail for help, but no one answered my plight. It was my "fix." I worked the stilt back and forth and tugged upward until it came free. Then I limped home dragging the stilts, while with every step the muck oozed from my shoe tops. The worst result from falling in the slough was having to clean my own shoes. I was supposed to know better.

It took the mop bucket full of suds and a table knife for the job. I slumped over on the porch, bucket between my feet, dipping each shoe up and down and scraping off thin layers of mud. It took time and perseverance; and, if I rushed, I suffered the consequences by walking on dry clods stuck in my shoes that blistered my feet and skinned my ankles. The leather turned out dry and stiff. It was usually several days before I walked normally again, much less ran.

At the end of the summer, a cleaner more creative time was spent with the three plays, which we wrote, produced and starred in. My play, always a comedy, was short and probably only funny to me. Each play had three characters, crepe paper costumes, and cardboard props.

I remember one I wrote about three clowns in a box. I didn't like to write so no one had many lines to memorize. The three clowns decided to go for a ride and climbed into a bottomless box and ran around in a circle. I wonder if anyone laughed, except the clowns.

The other two plays were written with more care—they had something of a plot and more lines to memorize. My sister, Margaret, wrote a mystery once, and it won praise from the audience. The other play, by our friend, was a western with lots of action. We wore our cap guns and holsters for that one.

The theater was the empty room upstairs which we called the playroom. We set out as many folding chairs as we could find, made hordes of tickets, and only sold four—to our parents. We expected to fill the "house," but only two came—our mothers.

These productions took days to plan, write and execute. The plays filled our time and except for the trouble I had memorizing my lines and a few arguments over who did what, the plays provided entertainment for both sides of the stage.

❧ PRISONERS ❧

I had dragged a folding chair to the edge of the road, and there in the gravel I waited for the army to come. My pockets were full of raisins and I was prepared to wait and wait. It was going to be an exciting time—a prisoner of war had escaped from the camp in the south end of our county, and I didn't want to miss out. I was positive the army had been notified of the dangerous German soldier on the loose.

As the war continued, month after month, year after year, the shortage of workers became more severe. Prisoners of war were used to help alleviate that shortage and for our area a small number, no more than fifty and probably only about twenty, volunteer German soldiers arrived to help log trees in the forest. These logs became telephone poles of which there was an extreme shortage, and the prisoners received the same wages as other timber workers.

They were housed some twenty miles from town in an old logging camp that was surrounded by pine trees, hemmed in by icy cold streams, and crowned by the Never Summer Mountains. It was a beautiful place.

At first the weekly newspaper ran articles about the new forest workers. I learned that a few spoke some English and that they earned American money for their work; but, most importantly, I read that they were guarded. I was convinced we should be concerned about these enemy intruders but most folks just wished there were more of them to work on the ranches, the railroad, or in the mines.

Once in a while I saw a few of them loading logs on flatbed railroad cars. They wore drab gray shirts and pants, which I thought were not befitting the enemy. I preferred black and white stripes. Sometimes someone bought for them candy, gum or pop; and before long they were an accepted, if isolated, part of the community.

A story circulated about a rancher who was breaking a horse in a field alongside a forest road. The prisoners were stacking logs nearby and leaned over the fence to watch. The rancher tightened the cinch, swung a leg over, and the fun began. The horse put his head down, arched his back, and commenced to buck. Up and down, round in circles, the horse was determined to rid himself of the rider. This went on for some time until the weary horse gave up and stood quietly with drooping head.

The rancher slid off the horse and to his amazement the prisoners cheered, whistled, applauded and said something that sounded like, "More, More!" They had the impression the rodeo was put on for their entertainment.

No one complained about the prisoners, but they had a complaint they made loudly—three times a day. White bread—they hated our sliced, white bread. "It's too soft, too light-weight, too white." "A man can't work on such nothing." "Ja, for the dark, rich, heavy bread of Germany."

As I waited for the army to come to find the missing prisoner, I was disappointed that folks didn't stand, gun in hand, guarding home or business. In fact everyone was doing what everyone did, every day—they worked. Sure the community was alerted that one prisoner was missing but no one did anything about it. The army didn't come; and, after an hour or two, I drug my chair back to the house where I pouted while I made myself a sandwich of white bread and butter, and topped with a sprinkle of white sugar that I filched from the sugar sack when no one was looking.

Before long the guards found the prisoner. He was sitting on a stump, just waiting to be apprehended. He wasn't far from the camp, up a draw and near the top of a hill where he could see trees and more trees, mountains and more mountains. No wonder he gave up.

At the war's end it seemed to me that the local enemy just disappeared. Eavesdropping at the country store, I heard that some of the prisoners wanted to stay in America; and, for all I know, they did.

⤜ When Nature Strikes ⤛

When lightning started a fire in the forest, the local men had to fight it. With a severe shortage of firefighters, if called — you went. The loggers were called upon first, as they had the necessary skills and knew the ways of the woods. Their hands were comfortable with crosscut saws and axes, and their feet adept at jumping over or standing on logs while clearing down timber. But if it was a large fire or spreading rapidly, the forest ranger called the coal and fluorspar mines. The ranger asked for any available men and then came up with a number, "Send us five men." The mines posted the request and asked for volunteers. My dad tried to hang onto his underground miners and crucial personnel in the mill and power plant.

After one such call two truck drivers, formerly from Iowa, volunteered. They were new to the area and had no firefighting experience. I was sitting on the steps of the office when, in high spirits, they left.

They were wearing new cowboy hats, and one had used a precious shoe coupon to buy cowboy boots.

I was sitting on those same steps when they returned five days later. They fell exhausted out of their truck, their hats were scorched and peppered with spark holes, and their faces covered with dirty beards. Most of all I noticed the boots. Scratched and scraped the toes and sides looked like old boots, but the worn-down, run-over heels rendered the boots beyond repair.

As the cowboy-boot owner limped toward the office, my father appeared in the doorway. Before he could say a word, the injured firefighter announced, "Don't expect me to volunteer for anything, ever again. I just spent the five worst days of my life." Dad hid a smile as he stepped aside.

"And if anyone even mentions a forest fire," the wounded cowboy continued, "I'm joining the army. I may be 4-F, but I'll make them take me. Nothing could be as bad as fighting fires!"

I stared at the boots as they disappeared through the doorway.

During that same dry summer, lightning or a careless smoker started a blaze alongside the road to Laramie. That day, when we went for the mail, a college student home for a two-week vacation announced he was going to drive by for a look at the fire. He was gone three days. We all knew the forest service was stopping cars to get help, but no one bothered to tell the college boy.

Lightning also had other targets, causing numerous haystacks to smolder and burn. It struck a barn, burning it to the ground and killing the milk cow and calf inside. That was a serious loss to the rancher.

My mother had a terrible fear of lightning. When she was a child her home had been struck, throwing the family from their beds onto the floor and burning a gaping hole in the roof. Also while attending a small country school, she had witnessed a classmate killed during recess as he stood under a big oak tree. She spoke of how the teacher rushed from the school to scoop up the limp body and carry it into the building.

Our lightning instructions were to come inside immediately at the first distant flash, stay away from the windows, and climb up on a bed or gather on the folding chairs around my father's desk. There, while the sky flashed, the windows rattled, and the thunder boomed, Mother, although terrified, calmly read a story to us. I rather enjoyed electrical storms because of their rewards.

But there was no reward for one lightning strike. Not long after my tenth birthday, a pond at the fish hatchery was struck. Located near the center of North Park, the hatchery was surrounded by rolling hills covered with rocks, grass and sagebrush. The area was known for severe storms, strong winds, and blizzards; but it was also known for its pure springs. The hatchery was composed of a house, several sheds, one fair-sized building, and three connecting ponds. I'd often stood at the ponds' edges, fascinated with the rainbow trout swimming in the clear water.

Following the strike, the dead fish began to float to the top. All of the fish were lost in two of the ponds; but the third pond was spared, which was a mystery to me. Upon hearing the news that the ponds were drained and over five hundred pounds of dead fish were shoveled from their bottoms, I begged to go see the piles of fish, but my parents weren't eager to view the carnage. Instead we discussed for days that strange twist of nature.

✦ The Picture Show ✦

On Friday nights we went to the movies. The theater had caught on fire several times and wasn't much to look at, but it kept us in touch with another world. The building, while fairly long, was very narrow with three doors—one "in," one "out" that was close to the "in" door, and one somewhere behind the screen. The movie projector was located above the "out" door on a wooden perch with a narrow ladder attached to the wall for the projectionist to climb up. There he sat on a folding chair. If the film broke, as it frequently did, we all turned in our seats, staring up as he frantically re-threaded it.

Cowboy films, which were my favorites, played on Friday and Saturday nights. Margaret and I went early to get a good seat, three rows from the front on the left side. Rows one and two were hard wooden seats, and those situated on the theater's right side were too close to the free-standing stove. The rest of the seats were a velvet-like plush with padded backs; but they had a disadvantage also, since many were torn and a stiff straw material stuck out-scratching our legs and backs. I favored a seat at the end of the row, especially if the movie got dull. By leaning out to the side I could watch the mice run across the aisle. The stove, a black cube standing on four stubby legs with a sooty stovepipe, stood in a prominent place just to the right of the screen. The front of the theater in winter was usually too warm, while the seats farther back required wearing coats to stem the chill. In summer there was one temperature throughout—hot.

We sometimes went on Sunday when something good, like Abbott and Costello or Lassie, was on, but that was rare because of school the next day. The better movies were Sunday, Monday and Tuesday nights, while every kid agreed the Wednesday-Thursday movie was always a dud. Since all of the movies were what we now rate as G, our parents had no qualms about our going. We walked around the block from home, and two hours later we walked back. There was no other place to go. The drug store closed early most nights, because the druggist didn't want to fool with a bunch of nickel drinks or ice cream cones.

The movie began with a cartoon followed by the newsreel. It was my least favorite part of the evening, but it was then that I tied together the maps on the living room wall and the radio broadcasts. I saw "our boys" blown up, shot out of the sky, trudging through jungles, and living in foxholes. I saw it all in black and white, fifteen feet away, on what seemed to me a gigantic screen.

I accepted what I saw, and while I had no fears, I vividly remember parts of those newsreels— the French women kissing GI's as they entered their villages; the body of Italy's leader, Benito Mussolini, hanging upside down in the square, and the Italian people spitting on it. Even today the giant mushroom cloud, boiling and blossoming far above the earth, penetrates my memories.

During one of those Friday nights, as I watched the bombs falling on England, I decided my life wasn't so bad, and I tried to pray a little for those overseas. And later when the war and I were older, pictures of the gas chambers flashed before my eyes. I was impressed with the piles of glasses, a tangle of metal frames and bows, taken from the victims and dumped on the ground; but I simply couldn't understand those trenches filled with bodies covered with lye.

I saw lots of war movies, some with singing and dancing soldiers and sailors on leave which I loved, but others were more disturbing. One was a story of ninety American Marines trying to take over a jungle island. In the end they succeeded, but only ten or fewer survived. I thought about it many times and was always sorry I had spent a quarter to go see it. It was probably a Wednesday-Thursday movie.

During the winter the same thing always happened. In the best part of every movie, just when the chase was going on, the theater manager came down the aisle with a bucket of coal. He opened the stove door, hurled in the coal, slammed the door shut, and returned to the ticket booth out front. By the time the coal dust had settled and the smoke had dispersed, the chase was over. Of course if the love scene came on, the coal bucket never appeared.

One spring the theater again caught on fire and smoke poured out from under the roof, filling the alley and cloaking the blacksmith building next door. As soon as I heard the fire siren, I was on the front porch. It didn't take long to locate the fire, and by cutting through the neighbor's yard, I was on Main Street in a matter of minutes with a first class viewing spot across from the theater and in front of the Red and White Grocery Store.

The thought of living without cowboys Roy Rogers, Gene Autry and Hopalong Cassidy was painful. I watched as the fire department arrived, and within minutes others had stepped forward to help a pitifully small volunteer fire crew. Some even came out of the bar three doors down the street. The smoke was thick, but I saw neither flames nor heard any burning, crackling sounds.

As I watched an amazing thing happened. A man with a long-handled ax climbed up on the old blacksmith building next to the theater and began to chop a hole in the roof—probably a volunteer from the bar. I enjoyed the new development immensely; but others, including the building owner, thought the situation was out of hand. Someone hollered up "Stop!" but the ax went on, up and down, up and down, up and down. One fellow tried to shinny up the front of the building to end the destruction, while the crowd forgot the burning theater as the "would be" fireman hacked on the wrong roof. He finally grew tired and quit, the theater was doused with water, the culprit—some smoking wires—was discovered, and the crowd drifted away.

It was over all too soon to suit me, but I could hardly wait to get home and fill everyone in. With a minimum of repairs, the picture show was soon able to reopen, and I forgot about the damaged roof next door.

One Friday night there was no movie. All the town's people were notified by the civil defense committee to keep their kids home while we had a practice air raid alert. The local butcher, our air raid warden, instructed us to cover all windows. Even our few streetlights were turned off. At the appointed time the fire siren sounded, and the warden drove around town with his truck lights off. Someone had rigged up a portable P A system for his truck, and if light escaped from a home, everyone knew it. I would have been horribly humiliated if an announcement had echoed through the streets: "Mike and Ethel, we can see light coming from your house."

In fact the wife of the air raid warden had allowed a sliver of light to escape from the bathroom window, and she heard her name blaring in the dark night air. Maybe I was "put out" because there was no movie that night, but I couldn't help thinking, "If the enemy is trying to bomb our little town, we've lost the war."

V. E. DAY
⇸ WHEN VICTORY COMES ⇷

Why were all the horns honking? What was all the noise? I looked out of our hotel window, but since my father preferred a quiet night's rest to a view, all I could see were more buildings across the alley. We were in Denver, Colorado, staying at the Shirley-Savoy Hotel, for the purpose of buying clothes and other necessities, while Father tried to find some mining equipment parts.

The 190 miles to Denver was a major undertaking, and one or two trips a year was it for us. To conserve on gasoline, the national speed limit was thirty-five miles an hour; so on those endless trips, I'd look out of the car window, thinking we'd never get there and wishing my father would put out his cigar—it always made my motion sickness worse. I know now that my father needed his cigar to puff on, as he worried that our threadbare tires wouldn't last until we got home again.

A phone call to the front desk to inquire about the noise brought the news, May 8, 1945, V. E. Day-Victory in Europe. The last months had brought a turnaround for the pins on our household map; and, since the invasion of Europe some eleven months earlier, they had been painfully moved inches, or even half inches or less toward Germany. Many casualties on both sides were reported in the papers, bridges blown up before the allies, and continuous newsreels of the bombings of Berlin. The momentum was on our side. I had seen the optimism on the tired faces of my parents and neighbors and had heard it in their voices.

Victory or no victory, Mother had a long shopping list; and my sister and I soon trailed her down 16th Street to the department stores—The Denver Dry Goods, May Company, and Daniel's and Fisher's. The sidewalks were jammed, the streets blocked with traffic, and everywhere, there were happy people. Some walked, arms linked, three and four abreast, through the center of the street; others stood on running boards, fenders and hoods of the parked cars. Cheers, shouts, and laughter joined the continual honking of horns. Many businesses were closing, including the specialty shoe store that sold narrow lace-up shoes for my skinny feet. I longed for black patent leather shoes called Baby Dolls; but with one shoe coupon for each member of a family, it was no time for glamour. After a few futile hours of trying to shop, Mother gave up with only purchases from Woolworth. By then the restaurants were closed, and I saw waitresses in their starched aprons out mingling with the crowd.

Lunch time and no place to eat—even the hotel's coffee shop was closed. Not far from the hotel we found a nut shop open, and to my delight we bought a large bag of mixed nuts for our noon meal. The Nut House, as the establishment was called, had put some folding chairs out front alongside of the building for their customers. We found two empty ones, and while Mother stood with the open bag, we dove in. The first handful was better than I had anticipated but, after several fistfuls, I was wishing for a glass of milk. I didn't complain though, for wonderful things were happening before my eyes. Servicemen were pushing through the crowds kissing one girl after another. The girls didn't seem to mind. In fact I saw one girl grab an airman and give him a big hug. I would have been happy to sit there all afternoon, but something told me my mother didn't approve of the lively scene before us.

"Give your chairs to someone else," she commanded. "We're going back to the hotel."

We pushed and shoved our way just like everyone else. No one minded if they got stepped on or elbowed. The scene in the hotel lobby was similar to the one on the street, and there wasn't a bell- hop or an elevator operator to be found, so we climbed the stairs to our room. It was a special day.

That evening the hotel's restaurant re-opened and, with a skeleton crew, managed to serve their guests. I was hungry enough to eat almost anything except nuts, but secretly longed for my favorite seafood cocktail. But there was no fancy food that night. The hugging and kissing had tapered off, and now the mood was more thoughtful, less jubilant. The sidewalk out front of the hotel was clear; the horns and bells were silent. Throughout the lobby, people sat or leaned against the wall reading newspaper headlines that glared with five-inch, black letters—V E Day. Our lives weren't going to change soon. There was still the war with Japan, way out in the Pacific. We had a long way to go.

✢ Seasons ✢

My favorite season was fall, except that school started in the fall and I wasn't fond of school. In North Park it was a short season but a dramatic one. The changing of green to gold amongst the aspen trees, the hillsides dotted with the deep red of the kinikinik, and all under the deepest blue sky of the year, splashed my world with color. The days were crisp-warm, while the nights were crisp-cold with a clear star-embedded dome above.

The creek was low, the fishing good, and haying completed. The haystacks still needed fencing, the livestock moved down from the high country, and the usual round of adult dinner parties and card games must be held before the winter turned mean. We all knew this exuberant season would change all too quickly to the somber one of winter.

Each fall Margaret and I hiked one last time from the ranch to the mine. This hike always took place on the day when the cook made doughnuts. About mid-afternoon we crossed the main road that ran in front of the ranch house and took the old road around the backside of Dean Peak to the mine. It was less than a mile, but the road was rather steep, rocky, and washed out. We looked down on the tailings ponds that caught the water coming from the tunnel and mill, and a few Hereford cows grazing on the patches of grass below.

The cookhouse, one of the first buildings we came to, was long and narrow with a door at each end. We entered through the door closest to the bunkhouse. Not far from this door was a small building with walls half way up and screen the rest of the way. Even the door was half and half. Two heavy chains, with three pronged meat hooks on their ends, hung down a foot or two from the ceiling. There was nothing else in the meat house, except the constant breeze that pushed past the screen. Surrounded on three sides with willows and low shrubs, the building was always cool and bug free. We weren't allowed to play in the meat house, or even open the door, although there was rarely anything hanging from the hooks.

Beside the cookhouse door, and *also* hanging from a chain, was a metal triangle—each side about two feet long. Made many years ago in the blacksmith shop, this contraption, named the dinner bell, called the men to meals. A long steel bar, leaning against the wall of the cookhouse, was thrust inside the triangle and vigorously banged against all three sides. It made a loud, ringing-clanging sound that, while not melodious, could be heard a long way off.

As we swung open the screen door, the cook, a small man who shook noticeably, greeted us. He had been the cook when my parents moved to the mine, left for awhile, and when the war broke out, he had returned. Since we made it a point to visit him only on doughnut day, he was probably waiting for us. We sat on folding chairs at the end of one of the long tables avoiding the benches that lined both sides. They were known to have splinters. From the warming shelf of the big stove, the cook retrieved a plate stacked with sugared doughnuts and placed them on a dented tin tray. He added two glasses of milk before he shuffled over to the table with our refreshments. He joined us as we told him about the trip up the hill and of any news we thought might be of interest to him.

While I stuffed the sweet, glazed treats in my mouth, I was amazed that the cook had perfectly shaped and sized each doughnut; and he never spilled a drop of milk when pouring. As the war dragged on the cook's tremors got worse, but to my knowledge he never missed a doughnut day.

Even as the gray of winter swept in from the west and the longest season was upon us, we didn't retreat indoors. We added more clothes including baggy-kneed heavy stockings, long woolen coats, and heavy scarves. The bulk and extra weight didn't keep us from enjoying the season.

Ice skating on the rivers started as early as Thanksgiving, when the nights were below freezing and there were still wind-swept open stretches of ice. Walking to the river with our skates hanging around our necks, crawling through barbed wire fences, and finding a spot of clear ice took perseverance. Later using a couple of garden hoses, the town flooded a vacant lot two houses away from ours. It was difficult to produce a smooth rink, but to my way of thinking, ridges and bumps were tolerable compared to river skating.

The best part was arriving home from school, pulling on snow pants under my skirt, lacing up my skates, and gliding over the packed snow down the street to the pond. There I skated with ankles turned in, and arms waving for balance. I visited and skated until it was time for me to struggle, points dug in, up the hill home where it was my turn to practice the piano. Even when the thermometer registered twenty below or more I skated, dreaming I was the graceful Sonja Henie. The skating ritual continued until the rink shrunk to a few slushy patches. By then I welcomed spring.

We didn't really have spring, just a time of higher temperatures, fierce storms that were brief but cruel, and longer daylight. It was then that I turned my attention to kite flying, a perfect activity for our windy spring. My kite was constructed of two thin pieces of pliable wood bent slightly to fit the diamond shaped tissue paper. To the center of the kite I attached one end of a large ball of string. The rest I wrapped around a stick, preferably one with few splinters. The kite was doomed without at least fifteen feet of tail made from tied-together strips of material found in the ragbag.

With our wind, it didn't take too much skill to launch a kite. I stood on the edge of a hill, let the wind catch the kite, and reeled out the string from the rough spool. Done properly the kite soared until it was little more than a fleck in the sky. I thrilled to think I controlled that tugging, diving, and swooping speck far above my head. By May the kite was faded, the tail heavy with mud, and the string grimy. It was time to throw it away.

Summer brought bugs, hay fever, and sunburn; but it also brought everything new-grass, flowers, leaves and animals. I often sat on the porch and tried to drink in all this newness. The mountains still topped with snow added colors of lavender and blue. How could something so old look so new? Even the rocks scrubbed by winter's harshness added a freshness. But most of all, summer renewed the community.

Every Saturday night the main street of Walden came alive when we all went to town. As soon as we arrived, Mother rushed into the grocery stores before they closed. She bought the weekly supplies while Dad got the town mail and sometimes a hair cut. I always hoped we'd find a place to park in front of the drug store. The kids congregated there, and sometime during the evening I went inside to spend my nickel on a chocolate ice cream cone. I stood four deep in the crowd behind the eight fountain stools, waiting my turn to order. Cones and cherry Cokes were popular as well as malts and shakes for special occasions. Meanwhile folks wandered up and down the sidewalks, stopping frequently to exchange greetings or bend down, arms resting on the open car window, to talk to the people within.

Some crossed the street, going from one bar to the other, or from the post office to the cafés. The mingling and music spilling out of the bars into the street produced a carnival atmosphere. But after the showing of the movie and the closing of the drug store, many went home. As our car pulled from the curb, I felt a twinge of regret but was consoled with the thought that another Saturday night was just a week away.

The seasons of war were no different from the seasons of peace.

The Seven-minute
✦ Disaster ✦

The occasion was a summer picnic complete with the usual fried chicken, potato salad and cake. Just your garden-variety picnic planned by kids and executed by moms. Only this time my mother let me down.

"I'll bake the cake," she said, "but you'll have to frost it. I won't have time."

"But I don't know how to make frosting," I howled.

"Nothing to it," she said, that fateful Saturday morning as she filled the kitchen table with the cake, rotary beater, frosting ingredients and two pages from a Big Chief tablet filled with directions. Then she rushed out the door to whatever she thought was more important than my picnic.

I fooled around awhile before attacking the recipe. I finally cracked and measured the egg whites, sugar and cream of tartar into what Mother had labeled pan "A " Next I got the water boiling in pan "B," and to these instructions she had added,

"Remember boiling water on the bottom floor and everything else on the top."

When the water bubbled in the bottom of the double boiler, I proceeded to beat the stuff on top with our rotary beater. It was a tiresome job, and I kept changing hands to soothe my aching wrists, arms, and shoulders. I also got hot bending over the stove and finally took the whole mess to the front porch where I sat down on a folding chair, with potholders and pans in my lap. There I beat at a more leisurely pace resting my elbows on my legs while I hunched over the frosting.

It seemed like an hour, not seven minutes, before the mixture took on the appearance of frosting. To my amazement it didn't take nearly as long to slap the white goo between two layers, dump some on top, and slather the sides. On went the copper-colored top of the cake carrier, and off I went.

Our picnics were never far from town since no parents had the time to haul us around, and besides they weren't about to waste gasoline on a picnic. It was a challenge for me to carry my cake and keep up as we marched down the side of the road.

About a half-mile from town was the Michigan River, a medium-sized river for our area, with a bluff above it on one side and a hay meadow on the other. I skated on the "Michigan" in the winter and fished it in the spring. I never caught anything but suckers, a fish I detested. With that gaping hole for a mouth, it was all I could do to hold it while I worked the hook loose. I would have thrown the fish away with the hook in its mouth; but since hooks were scarce and I lost so many on snags and willows, I had to take a deep breath, grab the awful, thing and yank.

The river was usually peaceful and always ice cube cold. It was deep in places, but I was never inclined to dip in even one toe. I couldn't swim. The nearest I got to being brave around the water was hanging by my knees from the girders beneath the bridge. That was one stunt I never mentioned at home.

More often than not we climbed the bluff, sat on the sandstone rocks, and told wild tales. We pretended there were rattlesnakes under the rocks, probably so we had an excuse to scream, even though we knew there were no rattlesnakes in our little world.

I remember an old cowboy saying, "No rattlesnake would come here where it is too cold for him to shed his skin." Then he always added, "I don't even take my long underwear off in the summer." Lying back on the sandstone slabs with our hands behind our heads, we discovered faces in the clouds. We fantasized about our futures. Our dreams were simple; we hadn't been anywhere; and our thoughts were rooted in the 1930s. After awhile we crawled off the rocks and found a grassy spot beside the river for our picnic.

I added my dessert to the blanket spread on the ground without so much as a peek. It wasn't until later, when we had depleted the fried chicken and potato salad, that I lifted the lid. To my horror the frosting had slid off the top, oozed from the middle, and surrounded the cake like a moat. Stuck in the sugary gumbo were numerous ants. The dessert was immediately named "ant-trap cake." While the girls squealed they wouldn't eat it, I stared down at my cooking disaster with a sick smile on my face. I vowed I'd never forgive my mother for leaving me alone to conquer a seven-minute frosting.

❧ THE PERFORMANCE ❧

I f you showed the slightest bit of talent, or if you had persevered with some type of lessons for a year, you were called upon to perform. In the course of ten years of piano lessons, I had honored the Woman's Club, the Lion's Club, the Rebeccas, the various churches, and even the Old Timers' reunion not to mention the many school functions. Talented, I was not; dedicated, only to the extent of my mother's threats if I didn't practice.

"Those one hour lessons cost a dollar," she reminded me.

But I did have some qualities that were missing in my fellow musicians. I played loud, with much gusto, and the middle part of each piece left me undaunted. Every piece had one, a middle part, where for sixteen measures the piece changed, and the original melody "sort of" disappeared. It usually changed keys and added a sharp or two or a flat, which threw off the most ardent musician. Then the tempo would slow and often halted, while the girl—rarely a boy—backed up or started over. Discord filled the air, and while the piano player struggled with those sixteen measures, the audience held their breath until the musician either gave up or skipped to the ending where the original key and tune reappeared.

My mother stressed, "Practice the middle part."

Of all the people in our community, my mother was the perfect model for anyone attending such programs. She sat up straight on the folding chair leaning slightly forward, as if in eager anticipation to hear the next selection. She had a small, approving smile on her face and a tilt to her head that offered silent confidence. "You can do it." Once in a great while, after a particularly stressful middle part, a gentle sigh escaped her lips; but unless you watched closely, the relief wasn't noticeable. Only once in over twenty years of attending did she ever falter, her poise threatened, her face pale.

Every year, in late spring, the aspiring musicians played for the Woman's Club. As a founding member of that organization, Mother was dedicated to its cause and loved the members. I was one of those musicians who yearly favored the ladies with my latest and best effort.

One year, for a reason I've long forgotten, I decided at the last minute to change my selection. I ran home from school, put on my party dress, clutched my sheet music in my hand and raced to the community church where the Woman's Club met. Since I had never mastered the art of memorizing, I had to play whatever sheet music I brought with me.

When I walked in, I noticed the tea table had a centerpiece of cut, store-bought flowers, which was unusual. The closest florist was in the next state, and by way of the bus, the ride often proved fatal to the fragile petals. It was a special occasion honoring a member who had recently past away. The program was dedicated to Aunt Nellie.

I arrived just as someone was reading a poem about a person who made the flowers bloom brighter and the birds sing sweeter. It went on and on about calm waters, gentle spirit, and ended with something about a legacy of tranquillity.

Then it was my turn, and I marched to the battered upright surrounded by folding chairs and club members. I announced I would play "Stormy Weather." My mother bolted upright, the eager tilt gone, the encouraging smile frozen. Maybe I should have stayed with "Waltz of the Flowers," but it was too late. I was committed and with my usual flair I began. It was a rather jazzy rendition, which was probably why I chose it. "Don't know why there's no sun up in the sky, stormy weather, since my man and I ain't together."

I was sailing along, when I hit the middle part. "Since you went away the blues jumped up and got me, the blues jumped up, the blues jumped . . ." I had bogged down. I glanced at my mother. That pillar of strength to all young musicians had turned to mush. There was nothing left to do but jump to the ending. With the last resounding chord, there was merciful silence and then strained applause. My mother's hands flapped weakly in her lap.

I was never scolded for my musical choice, and I probably enjoyed the refreshments on the tea table as much as ever; but I haven't forgotten the look of horror on my mother's face. Something told me I'd let her down.

❧ SUNDAY SCHOOL ❧

There was a time when I hated Sundays. Since there was no priest within sixty miles, and because the road between us and our assigned parish priest in the town of Kremmling was closed during the winter, we seldom had Mass. When we did, the two dozen or so members met in a side room at the VFW dance hall, where a chrome table served as the altar and folding chairs the pews. Invariably someone kicked a chair leg as we knelt on the floor and sent it sideways into the next person. My Sundays weren't idle, however, because the community church, run by the Methodists, needed someone to play the hymns for Sunday school. Between the weather, gas rationing, and the fact that most people worked seven days a week, church attendance was poor. While everyone thought the community church was a good idea, they didn't rush to fill its seats.

Many ranchers designated calves each spring for the church, then shipped them in the fall and gave the church the money from their sale. My dad wrote a check every so often. The ecumenical spirit was alive in North Park long before it sprang on the national scene.

The minister seemed to accept the handful as the active congregation and gave them "double-dose" sermons. I never knew of him calling on the negligent members to join the little flock more often, maybe because he was busy teaching high school in his spare time. It was his contribution to the teacher shortage, although I suspect he also needed the money.

Anyway every Sunday I choose three selections from a worn, black hymnal, raced through them once on our piano, and walked glumly to the old, white framed church-two houses and a street away. I wasn't excited about my addition to the moral well being of the community, but my Baptist-raised mother thought it was a nice thing to do.

I might have worked harder on the hymns and enjoyed my position more except for one person— the minister's child. I don't know if she didn't like me, or if she just bit everyone. It never failed! While her father was leading the congregation in song, her mother was putting out the Sunday school papers, and I was trying to play, she slid through the rail behind her dad and took a chunk out of my arm just above the elbow. I hit a wrong note, and the minister glanced over his shoulder as I struggled to find my place in the music. I hit many wrong notes while trying to keep an eye on that kid. This went on until summer when we moved back to the mine ranch, and I had three months to heal.

I often wonder why I didn't tell the minister or his wife of their child's eating habits. Instead I prayed we'd have Mass so I'd have an excuse to miss, even though I wasn't fond of those "on your knees" sessions either.

We all prayed for our servicemen; and while I knew most of the local ones I never saw them in uniform, something I would have enjoyed. As soon as they got home they put on Levi's and western shirts. They often spent their leave time putting up hay, herding cows, or helping out any way they could.

Finally the little girl quit biting, my mother decided I'd served my time, and I moved on to shower my talent on other poor souls.

✤ The Cloud ✤

If VE Day was so clear in my mind, why was the end of World War II so vague? The victory in Japan was more about isolated pictures in my memory than a day to remember.

It had been almost painful to watch my parents put the pins on those little dots in the Pacific Ocean. The map had so many dots, so many islands—the Marshalls, the Gilberts, the Marianas—so many casualties on Pelieu, Iwo Jima and Okinawa. There were marks on the patches of blue where the USS Lexington sank in the Coral Sea, and the battle of Midway where another aircraft carrier, the Yorktown, was lost. To me the war in Europe was gentle compared to the war in the Pacific.

I did love to watch the newsreels showing our ships sailing across the screen. They usually played "Anchors Aweigh" in the background, one of my favorites, and one that never failed to stir my patriotism. However the pictures of fighting to gain or hold some island were disturbing. Often I sat in the theater with my eyes shut. Of course I had to be careful; the other kids might notice and call me a baby, and that would ruin the indifferent image I tried to project.

I had decided sometime during a radio broadcast or a newsreel that the war with Japan would go on forever. When the pins skipped many dots, I was surprised, and when the atomic bomb was dropped on Hiroshima, and the mushroom cloud was shown over and over again at the picture show, I was bewildered.

Along about then my father took a chunk of uranium ore that sat on his office table along with specimens of copper, lead, fluorspar and other minerals. Most of them I could name and, when pressured into helping dust, I dusted the rock table first. He tried to explain that mushroom cloud to me, and I like to think, that for a twelve-year old, I understood at least part of what he was saying.

As he turned the yellow rock over and over in his hand, he said something about uranium being radioactive. Its atoms were unstable enough to create an explosion under certain conditions. He handed it to me to study, but I didn't see anything that might look like an atom. Still I must have been impressed for after that I put the uranium up front on the table next to my favorite, a rock flecked with gold.

Bombs, giant clouds, and suddenly, it was over. We had a subscription to *Life* magazine, and it was a weekly ritual for me to look at the many black and white pictures in it. I might read a photo caption or two but mostly I looked at the pictures. The pictures of the surrender signing aboard the USS Missouri interested me, although I thought we were being a little too nice to the enemy, and they seemed too arrogant to me as they stood stiffly in their black diplomatic clothes on the deck of an American ship. I thought they should shed a few tears.

I don't know what I expected, but our people appeared grim-faced as if we'd lost the war. Maybe they were thinking of all the people who had died just so they could sign some papers a long way from home. The only natural part of the scene was the wind blowing the khaki pant legs of the Americans. Wind I understood; it blew all the time at home.

The days following the signing were also confusing. I expected the stores to fill their shelves with all the things that had been scarce, so I rushed into the grocery store at the first opportunity to check out the candy counter. Nothing new there. No talk of a vacation, and if there were celebration parties, they forgot to invite me. What was it like without war? I couldn't remember a time when we didn't have war. People still went to work, still drove the same worn out cars, and still wore the same old clothes. I wasn't enjoying this peace and decided that peacetime was going to be dull or maybe frightening. What would we work for?

While playing softball, shortly after the war had ended, one of the neighbor kids said, "Your Dad will be out of a job. We don't need that mine now."

"There'll be lots of bums again," said another.

I didn't want to hear that. I ran home where I plopped down on the folding chair on the front porch, which was my favorite spot when I was in trouble or wanted to contemplate.

My Dad—a bum! I didn't think I'd like this peace thing at all. Would we be poor? Would we ever get a new car? My parents seemed more relieved than worried. Was it like the first day of school when you could never tell if the teacher's smile was going to last, and then it was the same as the year before—some smiles, some frowns. It always took at least a month to figure her out. Maybe it would take a month to understand this peace thing.

I decided it was too early to judge what was coming. Besides, the wallpaper above the radio had two big, clean spots, where the maps had hung. Mother was fixing my favorite, cornbread, for supper; and my father would be home to help eat it. I stood, folded up the chair, and leaned it against the house.

Bring on the peace.